MISADVENTURES IN MAASIN

MISADVENTURES IN MAASIN

BY

GARY ROBSON

Nipa Hut Press
Seminole, Florida

FOR AYENG AND DIDITH

IN MEMORY OF FE

Copyright © 2010 by Gary Robson

All Rights Reserved. No part of this book may be used or reproduced in any manner whatsoever without written permission from the publisher, except in the case of brief quotations embodied in critical articles and reviews.

Cover photo by Gary Robson

Library of Congress Cataloging-in-Publication Data
Robson, Gary, 1965 –
Misadventures in maasin/Gary Robson.
p. cm. -- (Nipa hut press)
ISBN-13: 978-0-9826682-1-4

www.nipahutpress.com

Printed in the United States of America

First Edition

Why I Joined the Peace Corps

When I joined the Peace Corps, I told my friends and family that I just wanted to help other people. There is some truth to that. In those days, I was reading a lot of Gandhi, and I spent many nights reflecting in the pages of my journal on a worthy way to live a life. I'd also become a volunteer at a crisis counseling center (aptly named "The Listening Ear") in which I took phone calls from the thousands of lonely and depressed persons who lived near Lansing, Michigan. In addition to Gandhi, I was reading Buscaglia's *Love* book. When you mix Buscaglia with just the right amount of Gibran, Krishnamurti, and Bach (Richard, not Johann Sebastian), you can't help but want to do something for someone else.

But there was more to the decision than just this; there was also the teaching. In my senior year at Michigan State, I'd completed the required semester of student teaching; afterwards, I wanted nothing to do with American classrooms. I'd found the right profession, but everything else was wrong. The books I had to teach from were boring and seemed to have little to do with life. The students were understandably apathetic, and that made the experience that much more pointless to me. The principal was an alcoholic, some of my co-teachers were clearly in the middle of breakdowns, and the rich kids of the school seemed ruined for life even before they reached my class. My overly positive listening-ear-type personality seemed to stick in the teeth of the school's cancerous maw.

So I wanted to stay out of the schools, and I wanted to help people. But there was something else behind the decision: a need to experience life more fully and more directly. The dead guy urging me on in this direction was not Gandhi, but Henry D. Thoreau. I owe everything to Henry. When I discovered his writings in the fall of 1983, I was a first-year college student pursuing a curriculum that led to a dream job: accountant in one of the Big Eight firms. But that was my father's dream for me; all I needed was a little nudging from Henry to realize that. With a great deal more nudging over the next few years (mostly from *Walden* but also from *Life without Principle*), I moved from would-be-accountant to English major and graduated in June of 1987 ready to begin my own experiment with life. I wanted to follow my own version of Henry's path, sucking out the marrow of life's lessons and testing each aspect of life for myself.

The problem, I found, was that the immediate environment I was graduating into seemed to be limited to one theme with multiple variations: make money and get things. And this held no interest for me. I wanted to live simply and directly. I wanted to build a hut, walk in the woods, study philosophy, observe what was around and within me, and record my impressions. This American life was indeed too fast, and if I stayed in the U.S., I saw that I would either have to run with it and so keep up with what I didn't believe in, or else stand still and be run down. Instead, I chose flight.

And so I joined the Peace Corps in order to escape. I thought that I might get a taste of what Henry had recorded in *Walden* by living in one of the underdeveloped countries of the world. At the very least, I thought that I could attain the simplicity in living that he valued so much, not to mention the two-year reprieve from U.S. life that the experience would grant me. I had made my decision in the summer of 1986, followed through with the stack of forms and applications and health certificates during the 86/87 school year, and had my assignment by the time of my graduation. In September of 1987, I was on a plane headed for the Philippines thanks to Henry D. Thoreau.

Bandana

No one signs up for the Peace Corps and automatically becomes a Volunteer. First, there is the lengthy application process, including background, health, and psychological screenings. If you pass through the initial hoops, you get an invitation and can accept or decline. Once you accept, you're sent a plane ticket to a pre-service training area somewhere in the U.S. (mine was in San Francisco). The pre-service training serves a dual purpose: it gives the participants a sense of what's in store for them in terms of a life overseas, and it gives the men and women a week's time to re-consider their decision to leave for two years the comforts of home and the ones they love. Each year dozens of people realize at these pre-service trainings that they've made the wrong decision. It's a good move on the part of the Peace Corps to have these sessions, for it saves them a lot of money in airline expenses (it's cheaper to fly someone home from San Fran than from an island in the middle of nowhere). Those who survive the pre-service training are given tickets to their country of assignment, and, upon arrival, they are confirmed Peace Corps *Trainees*.

The difference between a Peace Corps Trainee and a Peace Corps Volunteer is a matter of eight weeks. During their first eight weeks in country, trainees live with a host family, work in the community, and attend the Peace Corps training sessions on language, cross-cultural issues, and job-specific issues. If you can survive the difficulties of the training while simultaneously successfully adjusting to a new culture, then you'll become an official Peace Corps Volunteer and your real work will begin.

Training for me is now a blur. I usually pride myself on my memory, but the events – the new language, the Peace Corps sessions, teaching at the local school, my host family – it's all nothing more than a swirling mass in my brain: a hurricane of memories. All that sticks in my mind from that period is a bandana.

The bandana immediately became my main tool in the Philippines. When I went traveling, I used it as a washcloth; it did the job and took up little space in my pocket. When the rains came, it kept my head dry, giving me time to rip a leaf off of a banana tree for a natural umbrella. In the dry season, when I walked the dirt roads, a bandana protected my hair from the dust of the buses and jeepneys. If I cut myself, I had a makeshift bandage, and if I spilled something, I had a miniature mop. The longer I lived in the Philippines, the more uses I found for the bandana. But never did it prove more useful than during my first month.

We, the new Peace Corps Trainees, had just arrived. After having spent a few days in Manila for a health seminar and for vaccinations, we were sent off to Dumaguete City: the site of our two-month training program. On the afternoon of our arrival, the Peace Corps trainers and the Filipino language staff had prepared a merrienda – a party – for us on the beach as a way of welcome. I tried new and unusual dishes, got acquainted with the staff and the other Trainees, and joined a group for the beach games. And then came the rumble.

At first, it seemed like a general shaking of the earth, but I realized the movement was localized. Having been in this situation before, I was not too alarmed; but the rumblings intensified, and soon after came the bubblings. I began to panic. There was going to be a massive eruption, and there wasn't a toilet in sight! I didn't bother to slink off nonchalantly, but instead tore off down the beach to the path which led to the compound. There were around a hundred people on the beach – people who I'd just met and would be spending the next two months with. I wasn't about to dig a sandpit and drop my drawers; I had to save face. So I dashed for the toilet, about a quarter of a mile off. During the run, I made a back-up plan in case I didn't make it. I thought I could just whip on by the bathroom, run straight to the dormitory, have a quick bath, and then bury my drawers out back of the dorm where it was all muddy field. With everyone at the party on the beach, I thought I might be able to pull this off.

Still, I didn't want to shit myself if I could avoid it. So I pressed on, and just when I thought I wasn't going to make it, I was there. I burst into the stall while simultaneously unhitching my pants, and though things were in motion before I crouched over the seat, everything landed where it was supposed to. I'd made it! But where was the toilet paper? I had gotten so caught up in the race that I forgot that there was never TP in Filipino bathrooms. And so, within one minute, I'd gone from anxiety to bliss and back to anxiety again. But I calmed down when I remembered the blue bandana in my right back pocket. There was a moment's hesitation when I thought that it would not be prudent to give up one of my six bandanas so soon – my first day of training even. But since it was a better alternative than using socks, boxers, or T-shirt, I used the bandana and left it on the heap of overflowing garbage in the trashcan.

When I returned the next morning (this time at a more leisurely pace and with half a roll of toilet paper tucked into my pocket), yesterday's garbage still sat in the trashcan, but the multi-purpose bandana was gone. Apparently, some enterprising Volunteer-to-be saw the life still left in the bandana and with nerves of steal (and some form of nasal impairment) extracted the bandana, cleaned it somehow, and continued its existence. I don't ever wish to see that bandana again, but some part of me hopes that it still sits somewhere today – over twenty years later – serving some useful, but unimaginable, purpose.

Homecoming

After completing my training, I became an official Peace Corps Volunteer at a ceremony at the training site. Afterwards, all of the Volunteers were flown to Manila for various vaccinations and last-minute advice before being handed a plane ticket and left on our own to reach our place of assignment. As the only new Volunteer placed in Maasin (pronounced "ma-ah-sin"), Southern Leyte, I was truly on my own. The eight weeks of language training gave me just enough knowledge to ask basic questions – *Where is the hotel? How much does that cost? Where is the bus to _____?* etc. – but not enough to understand anything other than one-word responses. If the person I was speaking with said anything other than "There" or "Ten pesos," then I was lost. It wasn't supposed to be sink-or-swim with the language, but I soon found myself anticipating a drowning.

Getting to my site proved to be more of a challenge even than mastering the language. It took a cancelled flight to my island, a flight to Cebu (a neighboring island), a sleepless night in a cot designed for a tall midget on a ship crashing against a dock as a typhoon blew by, and a seven-hour ride over choppy waters until I finally reached a town on the correct island. While it was the correct island, I soon discovered that it was the wrong town. I didn't need to be fluent in Visayan, the local language, to understand the big sign in the town that was written in English: *Welcome to Ormoc.* So there I was on the sidewalk with about 100 pounds of luggage: a foot taller than everyone, painfully white, and standing in the wrong town.

The people around me just stopped and stared. I put my Peace Corps language training to the test by asking one of the onlookers the whereabouts of a cheap hotel: "Asa man ang barato hotel?" Success! The man went into a lengthy response throughout which I smiled and nodded my head repeatedly, having no idea what he'd just said. But there was that finger of his pointing straight down a side road, and that was a language I could understand. The finger turned out to be right, and instead of spending what was supposed to be my first night at my site, I slept with some cockroaches in a cheap hotel. I was up by 3:00 a.m. – the mosquitoes buzzing in and around my ears saw to that – and a short time later I was boarding a bus that was bound for Maasin. At last I was heading in the right direction.

Buses in the Philippines are not like buses in the States. Philippine buses are smaller – in proportion to the size of their usual occupants – and larger pieces of luggage are tied down to the roof of the bus. Inside, they fit five passengers on a bench that would hold two average-sized North Americans. I was skinny enough to make the five-passenger squeeze all right, but my six feet of height had my hunched over upper body connecting with my pushed up lower body; somehow my chin was resting below my kneecaps and my knees were somewhere around my ears. It was my first bus ride in the Philippines, and I knew right away that I had better find another way to get from point A to point B.

I was soon allowed to unfold myself from the pretzel form of yoga I had been forced to practice when our bus reached an impasse and all passengers were ordered off. After I had shaken the blood back into my legs and had gotten the circulation flowing again, I hobbled over to the crowd of onlookers to see what was up. It was a truck – a huge truck – and it had broken down just at the entrance to a narrow bridge. I saw on the other side of the bridge another bus with its load of discarded passengers who were staring our way and wondering what to do. Eventually the two bus drivers got together and decided to switch passengers, turn around, and head back to where they had come from. So while our luggage was transferred piece-by-piece between bus one and bus two, the passengers slipped around the broken-down truck single file and found seats on the new bus.

As I'd been warned in training about backpack theft on public transportation, I delayed getting a seat to ensure that my belongings made it safely to the roof of the new bus. Consequently, I had no seat on bus two. And not only did I not have a seat, but because the bus was three-fourths the size of bus one, I was forced to stand in the aisle between the two rows of seats and both squat down and hunch over while simultaneously holding on to a metal bar above my head to keep myself from being thrown every time we hit a bump. In this position, I was practically kissing my bellybutton – not easy to do at any time, but particularly difficult with one arm extended straight overhead, grasping the safety bar. And of course this had to be a public show. The two rows of benches were positioned so that the other passengers were all facing the middle of the bus. No one looked away in embarrassment; it was no little amusement to see this big foreign Q-tip performing a miraculous rubber-band maneuver.

After what seemed like days, I was allowed to unfold, only to discover that I was once more in the wrong town. It seems that bus two had come not from Maasin, but from Baybay, so once more I had to practice the language and pray for good fingers. Eventually, I found the transportation that I needed. But, to my horror, instead of a bus, all that was available was a jeepney. A jeepney looks like an elongated jeep – one that has been cut in half and had inserted an extra six feet of jeep. But unlike a jeep, a jeepney has a low roof and low seats. I figured that the only way I'd fit inside was if I rolled myself up roly-poly fashion. Fortunately, I found another way to ride. There were a few young men standing on the back bumper of the jeepney and holding onto the luggage rack that, like the buses before, housed the baggage. This was the place for me! I stepped up, secured the best grip that I could, and held onto the bucking bronco as it bounced over countless potholes. Other than the obvious spinal deterioration, the mouthfuls of dust from the dirt road, and the fear of losing my grip at every turn, this was actually the most comfortable I'd felt since the airplane ride from Manila to Cebu – and even that was no picnic, for no sooner had the plane taken flight than a baby threw up next to me, filling the cabin with a vomit smell for the duration of the trip.

After riding the bronco for a few hours, I was let off in the marketplace in Maasin. It was 10:00 a.m., and I had almost arrived. Outside of the market, I found a tricycle to take me to my new home for the next two years: Dongon (pronounced "doong-un"), one of the small villages outside of the main town of Maasin. A tricycle is a motorcycle with a sidecar that, in the U.S. anyway, would hold three people comfortably and still be considered legal. In the Philippines, three people are put in the front of the sidecar, two are squeezed in behind them on a bench about the width of half a butt-cheek, and sometimes as many as three people are seated behind the driver on the motorcycle itself. The driver doesn't leave until he has filled every possible space. It was on one of these, then, on a seat in the back part of the sidecar, that I arrived in Dongon.

The day was Friday and after the twenty-minute ride over a mostly dirt-filled and pot-holed road, I got off right in front of the elementary school, but there was no one there to greet me. They'd supposedly been waiting nearly a year for me (that's how long the process took from requesting a Volunteer to receiving one), but once I'd finally arrived, the school was empty except for a couple of children. It wasn't until much later that I learned that school had been cancelled so that all of the elementary and high school teachers could attend mandatory seminars.

One of the students ran somewhere and returned with the key to the principal's office and unlocked the door for me. I put my belongings in the office, walked back outside, and found about ten kids (their numbers magically increased in the few minutes that I was in the office) standing there. They all stared at me. Not a word was spoken. I knew that none of the kids in the area spoke English, so I tried speaking the little Visayan that I'd learned during my few weeks of training. But the kids were so shy that every time I spoke, they just giggled or hid their faces and ran away. What was I to do?

I went back to the principal's office and came back outside with my guitar (yes, as part of the 100 pounds of luggage I was hauling around, I had a guitar that I'd picked up during Peace Corps training) and began playing and re-playing the few songs that I knew. This brought the kids around me and after about thirty minutes, one of them got up the courage to say, "Volleyball?" This was the opportunity that I needed, so I quickly nodded my head and said, "Oo, gusto ko volleyball." So off they ran, disappeared, and then reappeared with a net and a ball. An hour later, hot and tired, I retired to the shade near the principal's office. The kids all followed me but still no one spoke. In fact, no one had spoken since that one word "volleyball." They just continued to stare in embarrassment.

I needed another icebreaker, so I went back inside the office, opened my backpack, and pulled out my B-flat harmonica (a departing gift from my cousin). I played a song, and the kids loved it! They asked for more and more songs, so I played and played until I ran out of tunes. After the "show," the children were much more at ease with me, and they began to introduce themselves. Imagine that: I had spent hours playing with these kids, and they didn't even tell me their names until almost 2:00 p.m. The kids in the Philippines are just so shy. "Are" shy, however, soon became "were" shy, for after the introductions, and some vocabulary swapping, and a little more volleyball, these same kids would chant "Gary" and smile every time I walked to the school from that day on.

Eventually, my coworkers showed up, and I wound up spending the night in the home of one of the school supervisors. Before bedtime, however, I was taken to meet the leader of our village. Mano Vidal was a very old man who had the responsibility of serving as sort of a chief or goodwill ambassador for the community. After we were introduced, he took hold of my hand and the two of us walked, hand in hand, all throughout the village. The last time that I had held hands with a man must have been when I was a small boy with my father. Still, I did not feel any embarrassment. Somehow it seemed right to be holding hands with an old man and smiling and nodding at the adults who were mostly too shy to say one word to me.

Whoever said that first impressions are what count the most was right on the money. I had made friends with, and was welcomed by, a band of children on my very first day. I took it for what it was: a good luck sign. Better still than the good luck was the attitude that I adopted as a response to this solo trip to my site. Things kept going wrong. I was either on the wrong ship, in the wrong town, twisted into ridiculous shapes, or standing in my village with no one to greet me but some kids so shy that the first words out of my mouth sent them running for cover. These were just the kinds of situations that were sending Volunteers home in droves. I could have thought, "How am I ever going to adjust to all of this?" But that never happened. All I can remember ever thinking during that time was, "Let's try something else" and "We'll just see what happens." *We'll see.* These words – this attitude – born and developed during my first trip "home" have stayed with me all of these years. Today I can't write a journal entry or a letter or contemplate a trip or an event without *we'll see* sneaking in there. That attitude is a great part of not only what kept me in the Philippines, but what kept me happy there.

Nonong's Hut

Once I'd finally reached Dongon, my first order of business was to secure a place of my own. The school supervisor that I was spending my first days with was a domineering woman who intended to keep a clamp on me both in terms of what work I was doing (so that it could be included in her own work reports to her boss) and where I was going. The first point I could live with, but I didn't want to be restricted from exploring the area; I was there, in part, to deeply immerse myself in the region. I wanted to make all of Maasin my universe, just as Thoreau had done with Concord, Massachusetts. And to go from a fairly protective stateside home into a cell overseen by a strict warden on the other side of the globe was crazy. I thought that my experience would be ruined right from the start if I didn't move quickly and find a space of my own – a point from which I could stretch my legs and freely move throughout my new universe.

I knew that I could secure lodgings in the town of Maasin. There I could have infrequently running electricity, unpurified water that flowed into or near my house, a cockroach-filled movie theatre, one rat-filled restaurant to eat at, or, if I preferred, any number of drunk-magnet dives along the docks. But these were luxuries that I could live without. I knew of other Volunteers who had either requested a site in a major city or who relocated themselves to a sizable town just so they could enjoy the same things that I turned down in Maasin. One guy even got a club membership at the Filipino equivalent of Gold's Gym and went into the city to work out every other day. I couldn't understand these Volunteers; I wondered why they gravitated toward the familiar when it was the unfamiliar that was most beautiful and interesting about the Philippines. Still, one man's ceiling is another man's floor, so I let them have their experience and embraced my own.

After ruling out the town, my first thought was to relocate above Dongon to the even smaller village of Lonoy. It wasn't just the hour's hike up a steep incline (a walk that the portly supervisor would never attempt) that attracted me to Lonoy. I had visited this spot with one of the teachers of Dongon on my first day and was excited about the conditions I found. They had no electricity, no running water, and very few people. I could get great exercise hiking down to the schools below in Dongon and then returning to the privacy of a hut at the end of the day. Also, as it was already in the higher hills, it was easier for me to reach the still farther off places from Lonoy than from Dongon. There were, I was told, beautiful hikes, rivers, caves, and waterfalls in the surrounding hills. I thought that maybe I could just take my things, along with a lantern, and build my own hut in Lonoy.

Just when I thought I'd made up my mind, one of the teachers from the high school, Ayeng Samante, told me about a hut that was not far from where she lived with her family. Ayeng was one of the few persons in the area who spoke some English (the others were the over-bearing supervisor and the aging principal of the elementary school). As the main English teacher of the village high school, Ayeng was also one of the persons I was assigned to work with. It might be a good thing, I thought, to have a coworker nearby – especially one who spoke English. In addition, I was troubled by a comment from Lonoy's barangay captain. A barangay is a village, and the barangay captain is the leader of the village. Mano Vidal, the kindly hand-holding elder, was the barangay captain of Dongon. When I made my first trip to Lonoy, I followed custom by going to pay my respects to that barangay's captain before doing anything else. As a part of his job, he showed me around his village. But rather than show me potential sites for a home, he focused exclusively on pointing out the single women. If he could arrange a marriage between a local and the rich American (it didn't matter that the wealth belonged to my parents only and that I was as far removed from it as the captain was), then he stood to be the local hero. And when I informed him that I had no intention of marrying – that I was just twenty-two – he made a joke about using me for breeding purposes. At least I think it was a joke. In any event, the encounter helped spur me on to check out the hut near Ayeng's home.

The bamboo nipa hut belonged to a man named Nonong who now lived in the main town and no longer used the hut. It had one room above the ground, a small porch, and a kitchen built to the side and at ground level. In fact, the ground itself served as the kitchen floor. Nonong met us at the hut and reported that its nipa-plant roof would keep the rain out even during a typhoon. He also pointed out an old water pump that sat in front of the hut which, after about a dozen pumps, produced clear running water. That was something I knew would come in handy since I would need some place to bathe, wash clothes, and clean dishes. But far more valuable than any of these assets was the broken-down outhouse set some 100 feet back from the hut in a secluded spot. While the thin bamboo walls were old and decaying, the toilet itself was sound, and that's what clinched the deal. Henry Thoreau could laugh all he wanted, but an old outhouse was the deciding factor and showed not only where I was to live, but also what I was to live for.

Chores

After agreeing on a rental price for the hut, I moved my 100 pounds of luggage into my new home and tried to find places for it all. Ayeng gave me a desk from her home, and she also helped the school officials to decide to donate two chairs: one for me and the other for society. Once I was settled in, it didn't take long for me to realize that I didn't really know how to take care of myself. The bananas that some of the teachers had sent over as a house-warming gift wouldn't last forever, and I would soon need to find both food and water.

Ayeng came to my rescue again. She told me what I needed to get and where I could get it. My first move was to make a return trip to the town. There I bought a bar of laundry soap, a five-gallon water container for fetching water, and a water dispenser with a spout at the bottom for easy pouring. I also bought one small cooking pot and a ten-pound bag of rice. On my own, I was lucky enough to find a shop that sold giant candles, and so I bought a few dozen of those as well. I had neither electricity nor a lantern at the hut, so I would need something to aid me during my anticipated midnight runs to the outhouse.

Back at my hut, Ayeng showed me where the community got its drinking water. It was an underground covered well that you pumped water from. I pumped until my container was full, and then I shouldered it as I had seen other men doing and returned with the water to my new home. At the hut, Ayeng gave me a broom and a coconut husk and showed me how to scrub my floor with the husk and use the broom to sweep the room, the porch, and even the hardened dirt floor of the kitchen. Later she brought over dishes – two bowls, two cups, one spoon, and one fork – and showed me how to make a fire out of dried coconut husks and other wood that could be gathered from my yard. For her final bit of instruction, Ayeng took me to the river and showed me where – and how – people washed their clothes.

All it took was the kindness of a neighbor – a new friend – and I was settled in. In a short time, I had worked up the courage and developed the language skills to barter with the best of them at the open market each week in town. I was supplementing my diet of rice and water with bunguan bananas (tender green bananas that were deliciously sweet), eggs, bread, noodles, and whatever fruit and vegetables were available at the market that week.

Later I upgraded to a kerosene-powered cooker to make my daily pot of rice. To get it going, I had to pour a capful of kerosene onto the burner itself and put a match to a scrap of paper half submerged in the kerosene. After this, I would open the nozzle, which allowed the kerosene in the overhead fuel container to be drawn down a plastic tube and into the burner to feed the flame. I had purchased this gravity-fed cooker from a shop in the town after months of frustration with wood and coconut-husk fires.

Besides the cloud of smoke, which filled the kitchen and sent me running outside, the main problem with using wood and coconut husks was that I was no natural fire-starter, and my ineptness regularly ruined my rice. I would use up twenty or more sheets of paper just to get the wood to burn. And when I did manage to get a fire going, I was inexpert at controlling its intensity, so that I always had more or less fire than was needed.

When the fire was too strong, the rice would boil over, and I would rush to remove the lid. When the lid was off, flecks of blackened starter-paper would float into the bowl. When the fire was too small, it would often go out before I could puff it up or cram some more sheets of paper into it. If the fire went out, the rice would sit in its partially cooked state soaking up the water until I managed to get the fire up some time later. Between the inconstancy in temperature, the continual removal and replacement of the lid, and the charred bits of paper, I was rarely able to produce an edible bowl of rice.

And so the gravity-fed cooker was a welcome addition to my skin-and-bones kitchen. My reason for not purchasing it sooner was that it spoiled my image. Somehow using something other than wood conflicted with my picture of a simple life and with my image of myself as a fire-starting self-reliant woodsman. However, an empty stomach won out over an empty head, and I purchased the cooker and lived to enjoy a great many bowls of perfectly cooked rice. Thoreau was laughing at me again, but it just didn't matter.

He wouldn't have had much to laugh at in terms of laundry, for while his mother or sister tended his clothes, I one-upped him by doing my own wash. Nearly every morning, on clear days, I could hear the pak-pak sound of women washing clothes in the river. The sound could be heard from far off, for it was made by a club striking a stone. The wet piece of clothing lay on the stone and was literally beat clean by the women.

I never used this method, figuring I'd get more life out of my clothing if I didn't. Instead, I scrubbed the articles, pak-paked them a few times with the palms of my hands, and then wrung them out in the river. My modified technique brought much tongue-clucking and head-wagging from my neighbors. They insisted that I wasn't getting my clothes clean, and they repeatedly tried to teach me the "correct" method.

Despite their open criticism of my wash ways, I was glad to have at least a few neighbors nearby on washdays. When I arrived at the river with my small load and found that one or two women were there before me, I'd always position myself about fifty feet downstream from them. This was because they had better eyes than I had and were more alert to the dangers that the river presented. The dangers were few, but they were disastrous to the unwary.

There were eels, small fish, and shrimp, but none of these posed a threat to man. Instead, all three had to fear the hunters – the men with homemade water-goggles and homemade spears who hunted the water life by day in the sunlight and by night with a lantern or torch. No, I had nothing to fear from these three, nor from the thousands of frogs that lived near the river.

My greatest fear came not from what lived in the water, but rather from what floated in the water. Once a visiting Peace Corps buddy spied something interesting while bathing in the river. He waded out to it, picked it out of the water, held it up in the sunlight, and then screamed: it was the remains of a recently skinned dog. Someone upstream, perhaps at the next village, had decided on dog stew for lunch and so after skinning the dog had tossed its remains into the water.

It wasn't only dog skins that were thrown into the river. Since there weren't any garbage dumps, the river served as the main disposal system. This was bad enough, but my village lay downstream from several other villages. Thus, garbage of all kinds and from all places found its way down to my stretch of river. But as the only objects that were really visible were occasional plastic bags and big things (like dog carcasses) the water actually looked clean, and if you'd never lived by it, you'd think you might like to have a drink from it.

But it didn't take more than a few weeks of living beside it to discover its secrets. And, even worse than the garbage, on several occasions I came upon children squatting along the bank. Not every family had an outhouse, so they made use of the river, thinking that it all flowed downstream but not realizing that the same thing was going on upstream – upstream in several places – so that nowhere was the water really clean.

Worst of all, the river was a crossing ground for farmers moving their water buffalo from one grazing field to another. When the farmers came to the river, they would often stop and let the water buffalo cool off in the waters. This was especially true on hot days when they worried that the buffalo, which didn't have sweat glands, might succumb to the heat if not cooled off. It was common to see one, two, or even a dozen water buffalo kneeling down in the river. And while they sat enjoying themselves in the water, they urinated and defecated freely and abundantly.

It was during the buffalo crossings that I was glad to have my critical neighbors upstream from me. As soon as one saw a gray-brown mass floating downstream, she'd let out a cry which sent all of us washers scrambling to get both ourselves and our laundry to high ground, atop the stones we'd been pak-paking on. From our sanctuaries, we would watch the approaching mass menacingly pass by, and then we would wait a few minutes – some more, some less – before resuming our chores. I always waited the longest before returning to the stream, fearing there might be one or two afterthoughts some few feet behind the mother lode. Yes, I could suffer all the criticism in the world to have my neighbors there, as sentries, to issue that warning cry when the danger was at hand.

* * *

All of my chores had me in great shape. When I was in the U.S., I used to do several sets of sit-ups and push-ups each day in addition to a walk or a jog. In the Philippines, I got all of my exercise from necessary work. While a T-shirt or a sock was fairly easy to wash, a person really had to scrub hard to get a pair of pants clean. Between the laundry, the toting of the water jug, the sweeping of the hut, the five-kilometer hike into town, and the return hike with arms laden with groceries, I was in the best shape of my life. I was skinny from the diet and the exercise, but my 135 pounds could hike and work all day with little fatigue. I sometimes wonder today how much better off I'd be physically if I didn't have a washing machine, or if I had to walk to and from the market each day to get my daily bread.

A Wedding

Once I had settled in and had a handle on my chores, I went straight to work. I was, after all, invited to the Philippines because of my expertise in the field of ESL (English as a Second Language). This last is a joke that any RPCV (Returned Peace Corps Volunteer) would immediately get. I was no expert. I was a twenty-two-year-old kid fresh out of college. My sole teaching experience was the three months of student teaching that I'd done in college, yet I was presented to the people of Maasin as an expert in the field of education and a teacher trainer to boot. My only strength lay in the fact that I was a native speaker and so could use the language fluently. The eight weeks of ESL training that I'd had was hardly enough to prepare me as a teacher trainer. As with the language, my job was sink or swim. I endeavored to swim.

It was a little over a week after I'd found Nonong's hut that I presented my first seminar to the high school teachers. There were three teachers in attendance: Ayeng (the English teacher), Mancio (the industrial arts teacher and the only male teacher in the school), and one other teacher who failed to appear at subsequent meetings. There was also supposed to be one teacher from a neighboring village, Bantig, who never appeared. The small number didn't phase me; I was there to do what I could with whoever was interested. I asked them what they wanted, and then I used the materials I received in training to put together mini-workshops on pronunciation, methodology, etc. During our sessions, I think all three of us improved our understanding of English grammar.

Mr. T, the diminutive elementary school principal, used to spy on the proceedings, which were held in his office/classroom. I say "spy" because Mr. T was always a little threatened by me, and he seemed unusually suspicious. I think he feared that I would expose him somehow – that I would tell the people in charge of the district that he was speaking the dialect in class and would only shift into English if he saw me passing by his classroom. Maybe he was worried that I'd report on his napping habit, which was extraordinarily consistent and which seemed to be based on morning, noon, and afternoon.

Perhaps Mr. T was thinking that I didn't have so much work to do – what with only two teachers in attendance at my seminars – or perhaps he was genuinely interested in bringing me into the culture, but for some reason he always tried to get me involved in things that I had nothing to do with. Almost upon my arrival, he was volunteering me for this or for that. At Christmastime, he had me dancing a waltz on stage with an elderly teacher – and not just as a part of the group but as a spotlight dancer. In the same month, just a few weeks after my arrival, he asked me to deliver the Christmas message to the people in the village, when he knew better than anyone that I was still struggling with the local language and so would deliver something that either no one but himself and Ayeng could understand or else something that was unintelligible to everyone present.

Just as he was suspicious of me, I too was suspicious of Mr. T. Everything he tried to do for me served to embarrass me in some way. A short time after I was in Maasin, Mr. T offered to trim my hair, and when it was over, I came out looking like a ten-year-old. And whenever he referred to me or introduced me to another, instead of using my name, he'd call me "the Peace Corpse" with the Filipino mispronunciation of "corps" as "corpse." He knew what he was saying, too. I'd see his eyes twinkle whenever he said it. Well, I'd only been in the village for a month when Mr. T, after spying on me during one of my teaching sessions, invited "the Peace Corpse" to a wedding. He said that it would be a good cultural experience for me.

The next morning, I arose at 4:30 because Mr. T had insisted that I be at his place by 5:00 a.m. I hadn't been in the country long, but I'd already learned about Filipino time (one to two hours behind schedule), so I couldn't believe that things would actually get started at that hour. But I was his guest, and I was too much of an American then to be late for a meeting, so I walked the paths in the dark and was standing outside his hut at exactly 5:00 a.m. There wasn't a light on in the place, and I guessed that either I had just missed him or that he and his wife were still asleep. I called out the traditional greeting which informs a neighbor of an approaching visitor, "Maajo! Maajo!" This roused their dogs and their neighbors' dogs, and soon everyone's lights were on.

Mrs. T, in bathrobe, peeked out from behind her door, saw who it was, called off her dogs, and told me to come inside. She said that Mr. T was still asleep, and when she turned on the light, I saw why: their table was strewn with empty rum bottles and tipped over glasses (Mr. T, despite his size, was quite the tippler). Mrs. T fixed me a cup of hot milk (loaded with sugar, as was the custom) and told me to wait a moment while Mr. T got ready. As I sipped and grimaced, I heard a lot of grunts and grumbling, some knocking about, and several Visayan words which I didn't know but guessed I wouldn't find in my dictionary. When Mr. T finally emerged, he was still half drunk from the night before. I was amazed that, in his condition, he was able to put down a large glass of sugar-milk before we left.

We took a jeepney into town and, because of Mr. T's delay at home, we didn't arrive at the church until almost 7:00. This, I learned, was no problem because nothing was going to begin for another hour or two anyway (Filipino time!). I spent those next few hours trying in vain to find a place where I couldn't be watched. I was still new in town, and, for some of the people, I was the first foreigner they'd seen. Thus, I couldn't escape being openly stared at. As embarrassing as it was being the center of attention in the middle of a church with nowhere to hide, Mr. T made it worse.

When the ceremony was about to begin, Mr. T made a big show of pulling me out of my corner and parading me down the carpeted aisle to the front row. He seated me with the family members and then took his own seat several rows back. Was he trying to embarrass me on purpose? I couldn't think clearly enough to know. I could only feel. And all I could feel was the gaze of every pair of eyes in the church on the back of my head. The people, I knew, were whispering about me, wondering what I was doing up there in the front of the church next to the bride's mother.

When the ceremony started, all of the couples (it turned out to be a mass wedding, with about eight couples, all around fifteen years of age) took their place at the front of the church, backs to the audience, facing the priest. Before any word was spoken, Mr. T was at my elbow informing me that one of the sponsors was missing and that I should take his place. I had no idea what this meant, but when he told me that the sponsors were the ones who helped pay for the wedding and who stood beside the couples during the ceremony, I told him straight off that I wasn't going to do it. But he continued pressuring me, and in such a loud voice, that now not only were all of the guests watching me instead of the couples, but the couples had even turned around to watch the twenty-two year old red-faced American argue in English with the five foot tall sixty-plus-year-old school principal. And so I gave in. I thought, "The hell with it," stood up, took my place beside "my" couple, and even signed my name as sponsor on the wedding certificate. And just after signing my name, the real sponsor, who I suspected had been there all along but was following Filipino time, came up next to me and from a foot away stared with the rest of the church. When I realized who he was, I turned to go, but Mr. T was there to herd me back to my place beside the couple. I was spineless at this point, so I allowed him to lead me back like a stray sheep.

The ceremony itself seemed to take several days. There was a ridiculously long sermon in the dialect which I couldn't follow. When this was done, there was a ceremony in which each couple was tied together symbolizing that they would be tied for life. It would have been interesting to observe and reflect on if I hadn't been in the scene itself. While all of this was going on, I just stood there like a massive sunburn. When it finally ended, I made a dash for the door but was halted, once again, by Mr. T. He took me back to center stage and somehow managed to get me to pose for a half-dozen wedding photos, for which everyone in the church remained to watch once they saw that I was on stage.

After the pictures, I rode back to the village in the "wedding jeepney" which was rented especially for the couples and their families. And at the wedding meal, Mr. T saw to it that I was given a seat at the main table beside the newlyweds – whose names I still didn't know. And the whole affair ended perfectly (for a disaster) when the food was brought out, and I was served before the bride's mother.

Critters

While the seminars were small but running smoothly, and while I was adjusting to the cultural curves of Mr. T, strange things were happening around my hut.

One night, I awoke to the flapping of wings. My first thought was that a gigantic mosquito had drilled a hole through my hut and was now set to carry me off to his lair at the top of a coconut tree. I'd had similar thoughts before and so slept with my flashlight within arm's reach. It wouldn't do much in an attack, but at least it would let me see what it was that was carrying me away.

When I heard the fluttering on this night, I grabbed my flashlight, aimed it at the spot where the fluttering had stopped, and found that my visitor was a small bat. He had flown in through the bamboo slats above my door and hung himself from the clothesline that was strung across the room for rainy-day weather. He wasn't in the light for more than half a minute before he swooped back out the way he had come in. I turned off the light and went back to sleep.

Ten minutes later the flapping returned, on went my flashlight, spotted the bat, sent him flying, off went the light, back I went to sleep. Until it happened again. And again. And yet again. Finally I gave in, let him have his spot on the line, and went to sleep myself. And in the morning, the bat was gone.

When he came back the next night, I didn't bother to play the flashlight game. When I heard the fluttering, I flashed him once, just to make sure it was him, and then went to sleep. And it went on like this for several days; bedtime came, and me and my bat went to sleep.

All was well with me and the bat until I began to think more about his visits. I wondered why he came in at night. It struck me that he should be out flying around eating mosquitoes and other bugs. Why did this bat go to sleep at night and fly off in the daytime? This really bothered me. I didn't mind so much sharing my hut with a bat if I had to, but I didn't want to share it with a strange bat.

And why was he always alone? I'd seen the movies, and in all of them hundreds of thousands of bats came flying out of their cave at the same time. They lived in flocks, so where was my bat's flock? Naturally, I didn't want them to start joining him on my clothesline, but I did hope that on at least one night he would flap in with a buddy or a girl. But this never happened.

And then I thought about his position on the line. He always hung in the same spot and in the same position: in the middle of the line, directly opposite my bed, with his upside down head facing in the direction of my own head. I started to wonder if he was really sleeping at night or if, instead, he was gazing with his bat's eyes at my neck. Maybe he was just waiting for the courage or for the right opportunity to strike. Why else would he forgo the easy meals on the other side of the door?

This last thought occurred to me as I was dozing off one night. As my sleep deepened, I began to dream. I dreamt of bats. I could hear them flapping all around, hovering above my prostrate body and feigning strikes. They began to descend lower and lower and, as they did, I squirmed and wriggled to dodge their strikes. And just as they were about to nibble all over me, I was able to wake myself out of the dream.

When I opened my eyes, I saw a great black flying object descending on me from out of the air. I screamed as it landed smack in the middle of my mosquito net. As it flopped around, getting itself tangled up, I continued to scream, and as the creature joined in with its own screams, I began to strike out at it with my hands and feet. This went on for several minutes, until the creature's screams turned into cat screams. This new development somehow brought me out of my witless condition, and I managed to grab my flashlight. The light showed that the winged, color-of-night creature that was struggling to get out of my mosquito net was my neighbor's cat. The bat was nowhere to be seen.

Apparently, the cat, which used to haunt the hut before I moved in and kicked him out, had found his way in through the berth above the room. He'd jumped to my bed – the only spot between the berth and the floor – and must have been fooled by my camouflaged mosquito net. Of course all of this was pieced together later. At the moment, I only knew fury and in my fury, I grabbed the netted cat, kicked open my door, and hurled him out of the room.

But back to the bat. I was so unnerved by my bat nightmare and my cat fight that I decided that the bat had to go. And, not knowing how to get rid of him except by burning a candle all night, I consulted Ayeng; she and her husband, Nanding, knew the answers to everything. And the answer to this problem was simple: get rid of the clothesline. That night, when the bat flapped in and found his line missing, he went into a mild frenzy.

He flapped all about the room, and when he realized the line was gone, he left.

* * *

When the bat was gone, the rats took his place. Rats invaded my hut every subsequent night. As soon as the sun went down, they came out from their daytime hiding places and met on my roof. I knew they were there because they would announce themselves by nibbling out a hole through the nipa. Once the hole was big enough, a scout would be sent through. As he emerged from the hole, I would center the foot-long rat in the beam from my flashlight hoping to frighten him away. This never worked. The scout – and those that followed – walked unperturbed above my head along the main beam that ran from one end of the hut to the other. The rats didn't even bother to dart; they sauntered along in the beam as if they were on a catwalk.

Sometimes I'd take a shoe and hurl it at the marching rats, which in their line on the beam looked like baseball-pitch targets. Immediately after the throw, I would jump for my chair in case I knocked one down and he, out of revenge, charged me and bit my toes. This, of course, never happened – not because the rats wouldn't make for my toes (I was convinced they would do this), but because I never got within two feet of a rat with my throws.

I'd grown up with a baseball in my hand, so it wasn't my arm that kept me from hitting the targets. I guess I just realized that I wouldn't know what to do once I'd knocked one down. All it would have done would be to anger him and to put him within a few feet of me. Who wants to purposely arrange a face-off with a pissed off foot-long rat? So I threw the shoes to save face. I had to do something; it was my hut, after all. But I missed by two feet to avoid a potentially dangerous mouse-to-rat fight.

One awful night, when there was dissention in the ranks, perhaps a squabble about who got to go in and have first crack at unnerving me, a row took place. The scuffling and pattering noises on the rooftop were bad enough, but when the rats started to shriek and squeal, I was frightened enough to spend the night on top of my desk, machete in hand. I decided that night that if I couldn't get rid of the rats, then I'd get out myself. In the morning, I informed Ayeng about my decision. "I don't know where I'll go," I said, "but I've got to get away from these rats." She said not to worry, to hold out for a little while longer, and she would find a way to help.

Well, I managed to make it through a few more sleepless nights and finally my "solution" arrived. It arrived in the arms of a boy who was accompanied by a few friends. Ayeng had spread the word that I needed help, and these boys answered that call with a black fuzzy kitten. You may have wondered why, when I first noticed the rats, I didn't get a cat. I'm sure my neighbors thought this. But I grew up in a dog family, and, as is sometimes the case with dog lovers, I was a cat hater – I'd hated them ever since I was three and had been scratched by one under my grandmother's table. And all I had done to deserve the scratch was pull its tail! Under any other circumstances, this "gift" would have been turned down with as forceful a "no" as I could utter. But this was a crisis situation, so I thanked the boys and took the kitten.

The kitten failed miserably. She was just too young and puny. She was only the size of my hand, and she mewed in whispers. And she must not have even smelled like a cat because her presence did nothing to deter the rats. One night, shortly before the Rat Hour, I stood on my chair and put the kitten on the beam just beneath the rats' usual entrance, thinking that they'd have a better chance to get a whiff of cat and so be frightened off and forced to find another hut to commandeer. But I pulled the kit down before the rats arrived. She was so pathetic looking – shivering and whispering – that I knew the rats would take one look, snicker amongst themselves, and then carry her off. So I took her down and from that night on, we spent the rat nights together – me at my desk with my feet up and the kit on my lap shivering and whispering. Things changed a few weeks later with another gift.

Gift number two was another kitten, and she was brought, like number one, by a group of students who had heard Ayeng's message. You might think I was foolish to take in another kitten after the first one failed, but by that time I was willing to try anything. My situation couldn't get any worse, I knew, so I took the chance on kit number two. She turned out to be my savior.

Number two was twice the size of number one. She didn't like to be held or petted but instead strode around the hut getting a feel for her territory. She had the appearance of an alley cat, a look of fierce independence in her eyes, and, thank God, the voice of a lion. She spent all afternoon trying out her lungs, and I was never so happy to hear cat cries. It was truly music to my ears, though it must have been a dirge to the rats, for they didn't show up that night. They must have heard her roars and caught her scent a mile off. They must have known that the master was finally at home.

* * *

Rats weren't my only problem, though. I waged a daily battle against the ants. I'd no sooner moved into my hut than my kitchen was found by their scouts; every single day I had a line of a thousand plus ants coming out of the fields, into my kitchen, and back out again. If I turned my back for a minute, I'd find a dozen in my lunch bowl. At first I'd toss the rice out in disgust, but later I'd just mash the ants in with the rice and eat them. I found it a fitting way to get back at them for eating my rice.

Once I thought I'd found *the* way to keep the ants out for good: I made certain that not a crumb was left anywhere, and I tied my food supply in a bag and hung it from a nail in my ceiling. This worked for one day. The next morning, I found a stream of ants going up my wall, out to the ceiling beam, over the nail, and down into the food sack.

I was stuck, and so I did what I always did when I found myself in such a situation: I called on Ayeng and Nanding. And, as they did throughout my two years, they came through with the solution to my problem. Following their advice, I soaked the string (which tied and suspended the food bag) in kerosene. It worked.

But the ants, for all their trouble, didn't cause me the most harm. I once awoke in the middle of the night to the sound of my own scream and violently scratched at my right hand for five minutes before falling back to sleep. In the morning, I vaguely remembered the incident. Just when I had convinced myself that it had been a dream, I noticed my right hand. I stared at it and stared at it, knowing that something wasn't right, but I just couldn't figure out what. It was only when I put my left hand out next to it that I saw that the right had swollen to double its original size.

I was certain it was a spider that did this, so I decided to show my hand to my neighbors, thinking that they'd be able to tell which spider did it, if it was poisonous, and what I should do to reduce the swelling. Nanding, the first person who saw my hand, said that it wasn't a spider that did it, but a caterpillar. I'd never heard of such a thing, so I looked for another opinion. But everyone said the same: it was a caterpillar bite, and there wasn't a thing I could do but wait for the swelling to go down by itself. And, of course, they were right.

On another morning, I woke up and found that my right eye was swollen shut. Although I'd been careful about checking my bed for stray caterpillars, I knew that I must have missed one. But when I showed my neighbors my eye, they were in unanimous agreement that it was the bite of a manok which had closed the eye. I knew they were wrong this time. I may have been a foreigner and a stranger to life in the hills, but I knew for certain that a manok (a chicken) didn't do this to my eye. How could a chicken mount my face without my waking? When I told them this, they laughed till they couldn't breathe. I, of course, with my swollen eye was not amused. When they regained their senses, they explained that they didn't say "manok," but "namok" (mosquito). I turned red and didn't say anymore.

I must have made the manok-namok mistake a hundred times since I'd started speaking the language. My neighbors would come over for a visit and I'd say, "So many manok," and while I scratched and swatted at my arms, they were looking around the yard for chickens. Or, when they asked me what I had for dinner, I'd reply, "Namok."

Anyway, they were right about the manok – the NAMOK. They were always right about such things. And it made sense, too. I was certain that I would have felt a caterpillar humping along my face, while a mosquito would just alight, inject my eyelid, find it had made a poor choice, disappear, and then reappear on a finger or a toe. And despite my future caution in avoiding the skeeters, I was to have the other eye swollen shut on a later occasion.

This kind of thing, by the way, never happened to my neighbors. Never in my two years did I come across a swollen-eyed neighbor and find that he'd been bitten by a mosquito. This kind of thing only happened to me. I was like a magnet for their greedy suckers. If I sat outside with my neighbors, as I did on occasion, there would be a cloud of mosquitoes about me, and I'd be swatting at my thong-clad feet the whole night. I never saw a neighbor swat at a mosquito. They weren't pacifists: they just didn't attract them like I did. If they'd realized the import of this, they'd never ever wish to change their beautiful brown skin for my white welcome mat.

* * *

But the ants, the caterpillars, and even the mosquitoes caused me less anxiety than the king of all insects: the cockroach. Philippine cockroaches are giant dark-brown monsters that do not die. I've stomped as much as ten times on a single cockroach and have had to stomp another ten when it's moved at the touch of a Kleenex. And they're so horrid looking with their skinny, razor-haired legs, their jaws, and those awful feelers which are moving in all directions.

They're also awful things to kill because sometimes, rather than scoot behind a table and escape, they run straight at you; they actually charge you. At first, I used to leap aside out of fear. But over time, I became so hardened to killing ugly little bugs that when a charge was made, I'd simply lift up the front of my shoe, keeping the heel firmly on the ground, and when the roach ran under my shoe, I'd simply step down. And then I'd jump up and down about ten times, making sure I landed heel first.

But the reason that the cockroach remains my least liked bug of the Philippines has to do with one night in particular when I awoke in pain to a gnawing at my elbow. As soon as I moved, I heard the pattering of tiny feet down the length of my bamboo sleeping mat. My ears honed in on the pattering in the dark, my body sprang to the site, and one bare fist smashed the roach into custard. I must have known that, had I taken time to light my lantern and get some tissue, the roach would have been long gone. And that was not acceptable – not after it had used my elbow as a snack. There's just something about a cockroach that makes its nibbling on my body a far worse crime than a caterpillar on the hand, a mosquito on the eyelid, or an ant in a mouthful of steaming rice.

Annabell the Cat

With the departure of the bat and the rats and with the arrival of two semi-domesticated cats, the strangeness was gone; it was replaced by a sort of homey feeling. The cats didn't cause too much trouble. They ate what I ate: bread, rice, or spaghetti noodles. Sally, the whisperer, would sit on my lap and whisper-purr; Annabelle, the lion, kept the rats away. For my part, I made sure they had some food each day, and I scratched their ears and chins. It seemed to be a good arrangement on all sides.

My neighbors, however, wondered what in the world I was doing with my cats and why I hadn't trained them yet. I had no idea what they meant. I'd heard of training dogs, of course, and had helped to train one once myself, but I'd never heard of training cats. I always thought that cats did whatever they wanted, whenever they wanted, and that such independent spirits would not bow to any master's commands. But Nanding showed me what my neighbors meant. He took a long strand from my broom, pierced a leaf with the tip, and then dangled the leaf in front of the cats. Dangling, the leaf looked much like a butterfly dancing through the air, and the cats went after it with a passion. My friend proceeded to show how one progressed from dangling the leaf in front of the cats, to dragging it along the floor and up the walls in imitation of a spider or a cockroach.

After that, I spent a few hours each day training my cats. Sally, the small and meek black one, played the game for fun and rarely over-exerted herself. Annabell, the tiger-like leader of the two, played the game to win and never tired. Soon, Sally was knocked out of the game completely. She couldn't compete with Annabell; also, Annabell made it clear to Sally that she was not welcome. And she made it clear to me that she was ready for advanced training.

I worked with Annabell for several hours a day, and soon there wasn't a cockroach or a spider that could get past her and into my room. When she saw a movement, she pounced. And when she pounced, she scored. She'd swat them once and then swallow them down, and this made me happy, for I detested cockroaches, and though I had nothing against spiders, the ones I encountered in the Philippines were big hairy goblins. These gargantuan arachnids carried quarter-sized egg sacks beneath them which, upon bursting, would send forth hundreds of tiny spiders scurrying in all directions. I was no friend of these spiders. However, when the lizards, my buddies, started to disappear, and when the frog music began to noticeably decrease in volume, I started to suspect that I'd gone overboard in my cat training.

Soon Annabell began to disappear for hours into the surrounding weeds. Having killed and eaten everything around the immediate area, she began to roam the fields looking for more prey. Gutted frog carcasses, 12-inch worms, and even baby chicks began to accumulate outside my door, and Annabell began to develop a paunch. I'm sure it was the carcasses that started me thinking about ways to deprogram a cat gone wild.

I was musing on this problem one morning when Annabell suddenly roared behind me. I started at the ferocious cry and spun around to see her latest game: a four-foot snake. Coward that I am, I jumped for the safety of the stairs above the snake. Annabell, however, had what I am convinced was a grin on her face. And with a light heart, she went for the middle of the snake and proceeded to chew through it.

The snake, not at all happy at having its middle gnawed on, began to strike the cat. But Annabell continued to work, oblivious to the strikes. Eventually, she managed to sever the snake into two pieces. Once this was done, she ate first one half, from the middle to the tail, and then the other half, from the middle to the head. Tears streamed out of her eyes as she crunched on the snake's head. When she finished, she let out a satisfied roar and dragged her sleet-footed, pot-bellied self onto the porch to lie in the sun.

After watching Annabell with the snake, I never again thought about deprogramming her. For one thing, she had saved me from the heart attack I would have had if the snake had been left alone to crawl up my pant leg or lick my toes. And for another thing, it was obvious that Annabell was too far-gone; no amount of retraining would ever take the tiger out of that cat.

Celebrations

Whenever there was something happening – and there was always something happening – I was asked to be there. During the first three months of my service, I was host of various Christmas and Valentine's Day celebrations; emcee of village and town fiestas; and official VIP/guest at beach outings, fiestas, dances, merriendas, athletic meets, classroom blessings, deceased body viewings, birthday parties, beauty contests, retirement parties, funerals, weddings, baptisms, and prayer meetings. The large celebrations all followed the same pattern.

First of all, I would wait at my hut for one hour past the announced starting time; in this way, I would arrive at the celebration only twenty or thirty minutes early. Filipino Time was the only time the people followed. I began following their clock after finding myself the only one present at scheduled meetings.

When I arrived at the celebration, I'd be ushered into the VIP section. While the "important" people had chairs, and while a few lucky ones sat together on thin benches behind the VIPs, the rest – that is, ninety percent of the village – had to stand. Who got to sit and where they got to sit was all a matter of social position. And when an important man or woman (i.e., a rich one or an influential one) unexpectedly showed up, a less important seated person would be approached and tactfully asked to relocate to a slightly less desirable seat; this would set off a string of seat-swapping, for he would then replace another, of lower standing, who would move and replace another, etc.

Two or more hours after the event was scheduled to begin, the emcee would appear on stage and introduce the main speaker. The speeches always began with acknowledgements of a few dozen VIPs, starting with the most important person and continuing on down the line. This took upwards of twenty minutes; at the end, the speaker would toss out a general greeting to those who had no standing at all.

The speeches were generally about as exciting as the acknowledgements. They were a string of clichés droned in half Visayan and half English – often with each sentence divided into a Visayan half and an English half. Unless you understood both English and the local dialect, you'd be completely lost. And as most of the people – that ninety percent standing in the back – hadn't finished high school, few of them could comprehend the English parts. The exceptions were the oldest people in the village who went through elementary school with U.S. teachers (before World War II, when the Philippines was a U.S. colony). But even these few were far from fluent and certainly couldn't understand the fifty-cent words the speakers invariably chose. It was obvious that the speeches weren't meant to be understood; they were meant to impress.

And this was just as well, for practically no one listened to the speaker anyway. While they all clapped when he approached the microphone, no sooner had he begun than the audience started conversing with one another – and not in whispers, but at normal volume. With the entire village gossiping about the speaker, gossiping about the Peace Corps Volunteer seated in the front row, or starting some new gossip, the speaker's message was completely ignored. However, as soon as the speaker finished – as soon as he said in English, "Thank you very much" – the audience snapped to attention and burst into applause.

Once the main talk was done, there would be a dance show. The performers – groups of teachers and groups of students – would take turns coming out on stage in costumes they'd been working on for months and performing dances which also required months of preparation. At first I was upset to learn that class time was replaced by dance practice for a program which was over a month away. Later, I realized that the singing and the dancing were ingrained in the people's culture, and I saw that the time that went into these performances was just as important – or more important – than anything that went on in the classroom.

The teachers who danced were almost always in their forties or fifties, wore traditional-type costumes, and danced traditional Filipino dances. They were graceful and lovely and obviously enjoyed every minute of their time on stage. The students dressed in modern-style costumes and did dances copied from the latest Michael Jackson video. The students, who were perfect in their imitation, had watched the video on one of the few TV sets that existed in the town.

When the entertainment was over, the VIPs were shuffled off to a classroom (most of these festivities took place at the schools) and were seated at tables – the most important guests at table number one, and so on. And while the VIPs began to feast on plate after plate of delicacies, the rest broke up into groups and gathered at a few huts to drink tuba and snack on sum-sum.

At these dinners, I often wished I was outside with the tuba crowd. While tuba (coconut wine) could turn my stomach, at least the sum-sum (snacks – often tiny pieces of fried chicken or boiled bananas) was good. It's not that the VIP food was bad, it's just that the "delicacy" most often pushed was crispy slabs of fried pig fat. While I was happily eating away at my self-selected portions, a rounded home economics teacher would turn up at my elbow and smilingly slap a slab of pig fat into the center of my dish. And there was nothing I could do to stop her, for in my village, it was an insult to turn down food. But while I accepted the pig fat with a grateful smile and nibbled on it whenever the home economics teacher looked my way, I kept a lookout for the dogs that always found their way into the school on fiesta days. Of course, I didn't get away that easily; I never got away from these kinds of situations. The home economics teacher would get me again with the "bring house" (the leftovers that were always sent home with guests). I'd often arrive at my hut late at night and inspect my huge sack looking forward to a late night snack, only to find a bag full of fried pig fat.

The fiestas never ended after dinner. Instead, we would all be hustled outside for the start of the disco. With the sounds of the music pounding at top volume from two six-foot speakers, the rest of the villagers – many of them stone drunk – would return from their private parties. The music shifted back and forth between discoish cha-chas (to please the over-thirty crowd) and 1980s dance music. During this part of the celebration, I tried to keep out of sight. I could dance all right, but whenever I was coerced onto the floor by a group of teachers, all the eyes of the village would be on me – the American – to see how I danced. I could usually stand this for about half a song before finding an excuse to leave the floor (going to the toilet worked best of all). And sometimes I'd go straight from the toilet out a back way to my hut, not wanting to be pressured back under the lights, under the watchful eyes of the people.

I'd hear the music for miles off. It would follow me as I walked down the darkened paths to my hut, and I could even hear it from within my hut as I lay beneath my mosquito net. The music and the drinking would go on well past midnight. While the people danced and drank, I eventually blocked out the disco sounds and fell asleep to the music I loved best: the sounds of the river washing over rocks, slooshing and plopping, bubbling along.

The Break-In

It was at one of the aforementioned celebrations that my hut was robbed. It happened while I was out at the local elementary school for the Valentine's Day party. I was the main speaker and while I was standing on the stage, microphone in hand, giving a talk about a day for love, three men from the village were ransacking my hut.

They didn't get much. All that the men made off with was a walkman radio, a watch, a harmonica, and $120. Nothing important was missing. The most trouble about the whole thing was having to put everything back that was strewn around my hut and also having to deal with the emotions stirred by the event itself; it's an awful feeling to know that strangers have invaded your home and handled your things. My hut was an extension of myself, and so I felt violated.

After the break-in, a half-dozen soldiers and policemen showed up, looked at all of my possessions, sat around mumbling together, and then departed, leaving me with the feeling that I would never see my stuff again. Still, I tried not to let this incident affect me any more than it had to, and so I decided not to change the plans I'd made to take a vacation to a nearby island.

I was gone for four or five days, relaxing, eating good food, drinking beer, and telling every Peace Corps Volunteer I ran into about the break-in. I guess it was not as easy for me to forget the incident as I'd hoped. And when I returned to my town, the incident was still on my mind, and I was even a little anxious to get back to my hut to see if everything was okay since I'd left.

When I got off the ship, I made a few quick grocery stops at the market, checked my mail, and then headed down the road for the one-hour hike to my hut in the hills. I'd just reached the edge of town when I heard a bunch of honks and beeps. When I looked up, I saw that it was a jeep full of the policemen who'd been assigned to my case. I waved and then moved on. However, the beeping continued, joined by whistles, cat-calls, and handclaps, so I looked over again. This time they'd stopped their jeep on the side of the road and were eagerly beckoning for me to join them.

My opinion of the policemen of the town was that they were a bunch of foul-mouthed, heavy-drinking, gun-loving macho men who would turn their back on anything for a price. My opinion had only worsened with their recent intrusion into my private life. I didn't want them on the case. I didn't want them coming around my hut to nose about or to disturb my meditations by asking the same questions about what had happened – questions which I couldn't answer because I wasn't present at the break-in. Also, I'd already decided not to press charges if the impossible occurred and the burglars were actually caught, so what was the point in their continuing their "investigations"? But they were the police, and they were on the case, so I walked over. Besides, they were beeping and bellowing so much now that people on the street began to stare at me. I'd already received enough attention from the recent robbery, so I quickly walked over to the jeep if only to shut them up.

Arms reached out and pulled me in the back and the jeep darted off, away from where I was headed, and we were half a kilometer down the road before I got a seat and was able to look up. What I saw shocked me: one of the policemen was wearing my watch, the second had on my walkman, the third had my harmonica to his lips and began huffing out obnoxious noises, and the fourth, the driver, had an ear-to-ear grin which he flashed every time he turned his head around and asked, "Are you happy? Are you happy?" I was too surprised to know how I felt, but to keep him from turning his head back and smashing up the jeep, I told him that yes, I was happy.

The policemen drove me to the station and after a lot of handshaking, backslapping, and chest-puffing, they let me sign for my stuff and go. Everything was returned but the money. While I got $20, $100 was still missing. The policemen said that the three criminals claimed to have drunk up that money. This, I knew, was a lie. $100 was the monthly salary of a high school teacher. They could have gotten half the village stone drunk with that amount. The thought occurred to me that the policemen were the ones with the dry tongues, but I kept that to myself. They solved the crime after all – and in less than a week. Also, I got everything else back, so what did I have to complain about? I'd soon have an answer to this question.

A few days after I had received back the stolen goods, I was forced to go through a re-enactment of the crime. Having learned that I owned a camera, the policemen were anxious to have pictures taken of the break-in for their files (i.e., for their personal photo albums). Thus, the three burglars were brought out to my hut and in front of half the village (how fast word traveled in that telephone-free town!), they went through the break-in again, tearing through the roof just as before.

Not only was I forced to witness and host this "party," but I was asked to serve as photographer, giving directions to the thieves as to position and lighting. Shots of the men re-enacting the break-in were interspersed with shots of the proud captors either grinning with arms around one another or looking tough with hands at their sides gripping their weapons. And while the victors had their photos taken, the criminals sat comfortably on the bench on my porch.

I'd suffered dozens – no, hundreds – of awkward or embarrassing moments during just my first few months as a Peace Corps Volunteer, but this "day of photos" dwarfed them all. I wondered if the king dwarf, Mr. T, was lurking somewhere in the shadows.

The Reconsideration Period

The robbing of my hut marked my three-month anniversary in Maasin. I was told early on by the Peace Corps staff that many Volunteers would leave within the first three months, and I verified that information by learning about the departure of one Volunteer after another. By month three, dozens had left from every site in the country.

Some left because their situations weren't what they expected. My closest friend from training left after seeing the remoteness of his location. He was several hours away from the nearest Volunteer, and he wasn't emotionally prepared to go it alone in such an isolated setting for two years. Another young woman left for similar reasons; to get from her site to any form of civilization involved a canoe ride, a boat trip, and a jeepney ride. Her isolation frightened her. What if she were injured or attacked? What if she got lonely?

Others left (and not just in the first three months but throughout the two-year contract) because of loved ones back home. Some left boyfriends or girlfriends only to realize that they didn't want to be away from them (or, perhaps instead, they were afraid to leave their partner on his/her own for two years). Some even left fiancés at home! Others went back to care for sick or dying relatives.

I knew of at least one Volunteer who left because the two-year vacation he thought he was getting in reality involved far more work than he had imagined. He discovered that he couldn't just lie on the beach for two years – that his very existence in a village made him a part of the community and that that in turn demanded he attend to the community. He was constantly invited into projects and other activities. He simply couldn't live in the village and go unnoticed. And so he went home.

Culture shock drove others away. Hearing another language day after day, experiencing unfamiliar smells, sights, and sounds, and feeling so estranged from one's "home" further helped to drain the Volunteer pool. While some could point to specific incidents – like not being able to stand one more time the sound of a pig being slaughtered, or not wanting anymore to see their neighbor's children doing their business in the river that the Volunteer bathed in – most of these leavers spoke of an overall feeling of being overwhelmed and helpless. They were suffering from culture shock and didn't want to – or couldn't figure out how to – adjust to their new home.

For some, it was just damn hard. Sure, there were Volunteers in relatively cushy situations – some even had set-ups not unlike their stateside dwellings, including a stereo system, someone to do the laundry, and even indoor plumbing and hot water – but the majority of the Volunteers lived a very Spartan-like existence. They had to bathe outdoors, use an outhouse, wash their own clothes in a river, fetch water, etc. It wasn't easy. When it rained – and it rained for at least six months out of every year in the Philippines – it was muddy, you were muddy, your clothes were muddy. Every day mud. And when it wasn't raining, it was hot and dry. Some grew tired of being covered in dust with never a clean shirt to wear because the river had dried up in the heat, and there was no way to bathe or wash clothes. They got smelly and dirty and had no a/c or even an ice-cube to cool them down. And so they left.

Health was yet another reason. Everybody got diarrhea at some time, and some seemed to suffer from it at all times. Those who suffered the most from poor health were sometimes medically released; the Peace Corps made the decision to end their service and flew these folks home. Some, it is true, benefited from the constant diarrhea or other such maladies. There was one woman I remember who had come in quite overweight but who looked stunning after a prolonged bout of dengue fever. Another Volunteer confided in me that part of her reason for joining the Peace Corps in the first place was because she was sure she'd lose weight. And she did – well over a hundred pounds, in fact. Those who withstood (or benefited from) their illnesses chose to stay; those who were sick all of the time and simply felt like crap chose to leave.

There was also a safety issue. Occasionally, Volunteers were mugged, robbed, or even worse. Pickpockets were everywhere in the city, and every Volunteer at some time took a trip to the city – for a good meal, or a movie, or to just get away from where everyone knew them. Once in Cebu City, while I was walking down a busy street, I felt a hand in my pocket. Without turning around, I reached behind me and grabbed the wrist of what turned out to be a small boy. Undaunted, he unfolded his fingers in the hand that I had an iron grip on, looked me in the eyes, and said, "Give me money." A far greater threat than these street kids, though, was the NPA (New People's Army) – the loose band of rebel soldiers who were forever fighting to overthrow the government. They were mainly located in Mindanao, the province immediately to the south of my town, but they made their appearance all over. They came so close once that all of the Volunteers on the other side of my island were evacuated. Although they were all given a chance at reassignment in a new location, only one Volunteer from that area accepted; the others went back home.

Some Volunteers didn't have a choice: they were sent home. These included troublemakers in general and rule-breakers (Volunteers were not allowed to ride motorcycles, visit NPA-controlled off-limit areas, leave their sites within the first three months of service, use drugs, or act in any way that would embarrass the government of the United States). There was one guy in our group who was so culturally insensitive and so obviously there for all of the wrong reasons (women) that he was plucked out of the group before training even ended.

With the isolation, the loneliness, the diarrhea, the day-to-day hardships, the physical threats, and the emotional traps associated with culture shock, it's easy to see why so many – half or more of my group – wound up leaving. The more interesting question, then, is *Why did anyone stay?*

I don't know about the others in my group, but I know why I stayed. I was happy. Yes, I had difficult chores, but I enjoyed them. I was playing out a Thoreauvian fantasy and learning in the process. Yes, I was embarrassed frequently, and I didn't seem to know how to do anything without the help of my neighbors, but that again was a part of the experience; it was how I learned the most about how to survive, about who my neighbors were, and about who I was. Yes, there were bats and rats and cockroaches, but with the help of a friend, these could all be dealt with. There were language barriers and work issues and a host of other difficulties, but I seemed to grow more from the difficult situations; I was forced to rise above myself and become better in some way. Both the language and the job were sink-or-swim situations. I threw myself into the former and, by the third month, I was genuinely communicating with my neighbors. With work, I transformed my tiny high school gatherings into seminars that included teachers from all of the elementary schools in the district. In addition, I started and completed dozens of material development projects, as well as projects with the college faculty in the town. I also worked on a book donation project that ultimately brought hundreds of books to both the school libraries and the town library.

Privacy kept me happy too. If I hadn't lived on my own – if I had lived with anyone at all instead – I would have gone crazy. I simply couldn't have done it. I would have been under constant scrutiny; I would not have been able to step foot outside the house without a companion (it was a part of the culture in the Philippines to never go anywhere alone). Having a private place to retreat to – my hut – was key for me.

The free time was what I liked best of all. Although I'd prepared and presented several seminars, in addition to participating in every imaginable cultural activity, I was never really swamped by work or by other activities. In fact, there were sometimes days on end when I had free time. I told a Volunteer friend once that there were some days when all I did was drink water and urinate, but that was just a joke. In my free time, I read (philosophy, literature, poetry, and history), and I wrote in my journal daily, recording the experiences I was having and attempting to make sense out of it all. If I felt like a change of scenery, I could take off down any path and lose myself in the hills. Actually, any walking I did made me feel good. It was beautiful where I lived, and by walking and watching, I was able to take in everything, and it all made me happy. If the weather confined me to the porch of my hut, I had lessons to create, letters to write, thoughts to record, and a guitar to strum. Life was good. I was learning a lot, and that was all that I needed to keep me anywhere.

And of course I had some good friends who I enjoyed visiting with and learning from. My best friend was Ayeng. She and her husband, Nanding, taught me everything from how to wash my clothes to how to train my cats. Ayeng helped me learn the language and Nanding, who only spoke Visayan, was the perfect person to practice with. They invited me – the foreigner – into their home when most of the rest of the villagers were still fleeing in embarrassment. I had my first Christmas dinner outside of the U.S. in their home with their family. With Ayeng, I could drop by and spend an hour talking in English about life, telling jokes, and just feeling comfortable. With Nanding and the other men of the village, I could drink tuba late into the evening, listening to the songs on the guitar, learning the language, and feeling like I was really a part of the community. I became so close with Ayeng and Nanding, and in such a short time, that when their fifth child was born in the spring, they asked me to be her godfather. So I was early on not only a member of the community, but also a member of the family.

I had other friendships that expanded beyond the small borders of my village – friendships which again helped to keep me happy where I was. I had Fe Mullet and Didith Espina at the main elementary school in town. Fe was one of the school leaders, and when I met her in January I knew that she was the one person in the town who I could work with to get things done. For most Filipinos, if there's a way not to do something, then it won't get done. For Fe, it was all about quality and efficiency. When I recognized this, I approached her and we agreed to work together. That's how I managed to present seminars to the teachers from all corners of the district over the next twenty-one months. But besides enjoying a competent co-worker, I also liked Fe for who she was as a person. She was a young teacher in the early 1960s when the first Volunteers arrived, and she had funny stories and fond memories of the Group One Volunteers. I liked how Fe spoke freely with me. She knew I could be stubborn and told me so; she joked with me; she shared with me her love of flowers and literature; and over long talks in her office and occasionally in her home, she brought me into her life.

Didith, or Dee as I called her, was a classroom teacher in the town school. We were first brought together for a huge village festival which we co-emceed, microphones in hand and on stage in front of thousands of people who had come from all parts of Maasin. We worked closely to create our dialog and in the process got to know one another and became good friends. From February on, if I had to go to town for mail and supplies, I made it a point to visit Dee in her classroom or in her home. She was intelligent, sensitive, and she had the voice of an angel. She taught me how to strum all of the Visayan songs that I know. Through Dee's efforts, I was later invited both to lecture to the college students in town and to present seminars to the college faculty.

Ayeng, Fe, and Dee: these were my three stars. Most of my learnings and all of my laughter came through these women. Born and raised in three different villages in the middle of nowhere, they were the kindest, most intelligent, and most generous souls I have ever encountered. They were my friends, and they were why I stayed.

All that I have outlined here made me forget about the ants, the mosquitoes, the rats, and any other "inconvenience" which might have made my stay anything less than perfect. As things stood, I wouldn't have changed a thing about where and how I was living. I had a home, a place in a community, and three good friends. Life was never better.

The Walk to Town

When the three-month "reconsideration period" ended, I marked its passing but did nothing. I wasn't going anywhere, and I was too busy living my days to give it much thought. I had the chores to do, the new seminars for the elementary teachers to create, and the supplies to purchase. This last task involved a walk to town.

My reasons for going to town were varied. I depended on the market for all of my food needs. Although I'd planted a garden shortly after I moved into Nonong's hut, the plot yielded nothing but eggplant (which I did not eat even though I planted it) and marble-sized tomatoes. I had planted sweet corn and was expecting to live off of it, but the neighbors' pigs, which wandered wildly (as did everyone's livestock), got to the young shoots before they could grow. I used to collect rocks from my yard and store them on my porch so that I could throw them at the invading pigs. I had a good view from the porch, and I had a lot of success nailing the pigs in the ass and scaring them off. But as the pigs were persistent, and as I was not always in my hut to watch for them, they eventually got every shoot – and not only from the initial planting but from all subsequent plantings. I was relating my battle with the pigs once to a Volunteer friend during a vacation to Cebu when he interrupted to ask, "Why didn't you just put a pen around your corn?" I replied without missing a beat, "Because I like throwing rocks at the pigs." And it was true. It wasn't until I said it aloud without thought that I realized that I had had more enjoyment from battling the pigs than I would have had from the sweet corn.

In any event, my depleted garden had little to offer me in terms of meals, and even though my neighbors – especially Ayeng – were often bringing me boiled bananas, coconuts, or stew, I still needed the market. I lived on rice and bananas, so these were my regular purchases. But I also occasionally bought potatoes and a variety of fruit, such as lanzones, mangoes, pineapples, starfruit, water-apples – whatever happened to be in season at the time. I also had a favorite bakery where I would buy banana cake. And there was one small supermarket – aside from the open market

– where I bought the peanuts and raisins which I kept on hand as emergency rations and as a variation to my regular diet.

Sometimes I ate in town. I had two main hangouts – one was primarily for food, and the other was more for relaxation (though I ate there too). The first hangout, a nameless one-room dive beside the pier, served ginomay – a simple beef and potato stew which was delicious. I was strictly vegetarian (if you don't count ants) out at my hut, so I walked into town and ate ginomay whenever my body craved meat. The second place could probably be considered a real restaurant. It was a large enclosed building with dozens of tables and a kitchen out back. They even had a second floor, a stage for nighttime performances, a TV in the corner, and, most importantly, a toilet. This was the only place in town that I knew of that had a toilet. I'd sometimes go inside, order a cheese and onion omelet, and make use of the facilities.

Thoreau had his occasional meals in town with the Emersons and with his family; I had Baltavian's Restaurant, and instead of the Emersons, I had the Gallahers who lived a good two hours' hike from my hut. Brenda and Steve were the only other Volunteers in my area. They had been assigned nearly two years before me as part of an agro-forestry group, and they would leave just a few months after my arrival. We met at Baltavian's every two weeks to hang out, share experiences, and relax. They were what I called "hermit Volunteers" – those who stay in their hut and rarely come out. They had found an old couple outside of the town with whom they felt comfortable, and they spent their two years in an adjacent hut, working only with that couple and basically just puttering around their own hut. I liked seeing them in town, though, because Steve drank beer, and every once in a while I enjoyed getting drunk and watching the Rambo-type videos Mr. Baltavian showed on the TV in the corner of the restaurant. Steve and Brenda, the beer, and the videos were my only link to home. They represented less than one-tenth of one percent of my Peace Corps experience, but I was glad to have them.

Of everything, though, it was the mail that was my main reason for coming into town. I could live on bananas and water and go without meat or beer or videos for a month, but I had to get my mail. I was rarely happier than when I entered the post office and was presented with three or four letters. Any mail was good mail, and it sustained my spirit like blood did my heart. Mail brought news from home – both death reports and, far more frequently, life reports. Letters from friends brought back memories and helped me to reflect on my current lifestyle – to see what I had given up and what I had gained. Letters from other Peace Corps Volunteers – which told who had quit, who was about to quit, and who was thriving – added to my own resolve to finish my two-year contract. Every letter I received was a good one – even the bad ones.

Other reasons for going to town were either school-related (such as a meeting, a seminar, or a celebration) or community-related (such as a funeral, a wedding, or a village fiesta). I was often asked to speak at the big fiestas, and I even served as emcee on occasion, splashing my comments with Visayan, which I was quickly learning.

Friends, too, were a reason for going to town. There was Tsu-kee, a Philippine-born Chinese who ran the best all-purpose store in town. Although he grew up not far from Maasin, he spoke very good English, having learned it, he said, by watching movies. He was one of the few Chinese in town and one of the wealthiest men, so he was a bit of an outsider, like myself. And as he was about my age and extremely kind and likable, I'd stop by his shop and chat with him whenever I went to town. Dee, the elementary school teacher, was there for philosophical discussions and music lessons. And Fe was there too. Fe was a fountain of wisdom and a symbol of purposeful living. Whenever I could find her alone in her office, I'd make myself at home and take up her time.

The market, the mail, and the friends were all of the reasons for a walk into town, and to make that walk, I had to go through a series of Herculean tasks. First, I had to pass through a gauntlet of neighbors and their greeting: Asa man ka? (Where are you going?) Everyone I met greeted me in this way, and so I would have to announce to everyone that I was on my way to town. This got boring fast, and over time I began to vary my responses. Often I'd answer their question with "To the moon" or "To China" or "To your house for dinner." It hardly mattered what I said, though, just as no one in the U.S. notices when someone answers, "How are you?" with a list of devastating ailments. Instead, we smile and say something like, "All right then. See you later."

Once I'd passed the Q-and-A part of the walk, I was on the main road to town. The main road was an up and down series of hills which was a river of mud in the rainy season and a cloud of dust during the other six months of the year. Besides the elements themselves, my main enemies were passing jeepneys, which would either paint me with mud or coat me with dust. Although I always walked the fastest along this stretch of road so that I could make it to the turn-off path still clean, I was rarely successful.

The small path, which turned from the road and led to the river, passed through one tiny collection of huts. The men who lived here were called "stand-bys" – jobless men who were supposedly standing by waiting for work. In the two years that I passed by, I never saw these men do anything but sit, drink, or spit; they were on permanent standby. Every time I approached this group, they invited me to get drunk with them. And for two years, I politely declined and continued on my way.

The path ended at the bank of a river. Here I'd remove my shoes and socks, roll up my pant legs (to below the knee in the dry season and to as high as I could hike them in the wet season) and cross the stream. It wasn't so hard wading across because most of the stones had been removed by women workers who received a few pennies for every bag of stones they delivered to the construction companies in town.

Once across the river, I'd dry my feet with the tops of my socks and then replace wet socks and shoes and continue my walk. The next path I followed ran through a coconut grove. This was the best part of my walk, for it was shady and cool under all of those trees. Although there was the occasional call of "Hey, Joe!" from a manangiti (tuba wine gatherer) at the top of a coconut tree, there was little else to disturb me save the startling thump of a fallen coconut. This path wound its way through the grove and made its way up a hill to a small village. I'd walk through the village shouting "Labi sa ako" – a greeting which informed the people that somebody was passing by. The children would all run out and follow me as I walked down the path, laughing at my "tall" nose and imitating my giant strides. I'd hear their shouts of "Bye!" or "Give me one peso!" as I made my way beyond the end of their huts.

Once past this village, it was just a few hundred feet to the outer edge of town. And from the edge all the way to the center, the calm of the coconut grove was replaced by dozens and dozens of honking pedicabs, jeepneys, and buses. The houses here were even different – mostly concrete, hot, and ugly. The air was worse, and there were a number of mangy dogs creeping all around. It was my least favorite place, and I was glad that I lived an hour away up in the slow villages, in the cool tree-filled hills.

Haircut

Once I made the walk to town for a haircut. It had been about four months since Mr. T's ten-year-old styling, and it was time to find a barber. I had no problem locating the barbershop in the center of everything. The barber (there was only one) was already cutting someone's hair so I told him I'd come back in twenty minutes. Before leaving, however, I checked out the haircut he was giving his customer, and, since it looked okay, I decided to go back.

When I returned to the barbershop, the barber wasn't there. Instead, I met an ancient man who asked me to take a seat in one of the chairs. Then he proceeded to wrap a ragged piece of cloth around my neck and sharpen his scissors on a piece of wood. I had nothing against this guy, of course, but he was really old, and I wasn't so sure how well he could cut hair. I at least saw the other guy, but I had no information on the great-grandfather who had replaced him. Before he had a chance to start, I asked him where his partner was. He said he was out eating somewhere and wouldn't be back for a few hours. Since I didn't want to wait that long, I figured I'd take a chance and let this guy cut my hair. I have never been more nervous during a haircut.

First of all, he had a pair of right-handed scissors in his left hand. Secondly, his right hand – the comb hand – was shaking up and down like popcorn in a popper. The old man picked up a dirty white comb which he'd probably been using since 1942 – and without having ever cleaned the thing! – and he proceeded to comb my hair. Then he "shaked" up a bunch of hair with his shaker of a hand and snipped part of it off. He did this all around my head several times, and never once did he evenly cut one bunch of hair. When he tried to cut the top of my hair, he had to stand on his tiptoes and extend his arms practically straight up – and even then he still couldn't get at my hair at any kind of an even angle. This chopping went on for several minutes; then finally he stopped. I was overjoyed to find that both my ears were still attached to my head. But then he picked up a razor blade – the old-fashioned kind – and began sharpening it on his block of wood, and I began to get nervous again – really nervous.

Before taking the razor to me, he picked up a dirty piece of paper – which had obviously been handled several times in the past several weeks – dipped it into a cup of brown water, and then rubbed it all over my head and the back of my neck. Next he reached for his dirty comb to comb my hair but dropped it in a pile of hair and dust on the floor. That didn't bother him any; he just picked the comb up and took it directly from the hairballs on the floor to my head. I stifled a scream.

After combing my hair for a minute or two, he took the razor blade – *in his shaky hand* – and began scraping the back of my neck. He didn't finish until he had scraped my neck bare along with the areas above and behind my ears. He also scraped parts of my hair, randomly, until he seemed to tire of all the scraping and finally threw his razor on the counter in front of him. I can't really describe any better the razor-cutting portion of the haircut; my mind seemed to freeze with fear. All I can recall is that I somehow didn't bleed, and I was able to stand up, without assistance, and walk out of the barbershop. After my time in the hands of Shaky McBlade, I never again made the walk into town for a haircut.

Bugas

Summer vacation, which began in March and ended in June, took place during part of the dry season. Thus, when my first March rolled around, I had nowhere to present my seminars and no one to present them to. I was free for the summer! Included among my other summer goals of hiking, reading, and studying the language, was the goal of eliminating the bugas.

The first time someone looked at me and said, "Naay bugas," I thought they were crazy. Translated, the sentence means, "You have uncooked white rice." I thought it was bizarre for someone to say this on the road to town, at the library, in the sea – anywhere, that is, except in the kitchen, where such a sentence should have been uttered. And the longer I lived in the village, the more often someone approached me and said, "Naay bugas." When I began to hear the comment on a daily basis, I decided to find out just what it meant; obviously, it held a greater significance than I'd originally thought.

The answers to most of my language problems were found in a huge Visayan dictionary I'd borrowed from the Peace Corps library in Cebu. When I looked up "bugas," I found my answer. "Bugas" did indeed mean "uncooked white rice," but it also had a secondary, slang, definition: acne. There was no need to look for a third definition. I'd had bugas as a teenager, but when I left for the Philippines, I'd long since been given my clearance papers from my dermatologist. However, the hot and humid temperatures of my island brought it back. And so at twenty-two years of age, I still had to endure the plague of my teens.

The Filipinos' insensitivity to my condition made it less bearable. I tried not to hold this against them, though, because I'd long since observed that it was a part of their culture to comment on physical flaws. Several times I'd heard one person say to another, even a woman, "Hey, you're fat." And often the first comment of anyone encountering me on the street was a loud exclamation of, "Uy! Taas ang ilong!" or "Wow! That's a big nose!" This, of course, was immediately followed by, "Naay bugas."

Certainly I didn't like being told I had bugas, and I liked even less actually having them. My neighbors must not have liked them either, for they began to follow their "Naay bugas" comments with guaranteed cures.

After a time, I learned that there were two main cures for bugas that most villagers stood by. The first was to wash with a local soap that was usually used for laundry. As the brand they mentioned happened to be the kind I had for my clothes, I used a bar to wash my face with, twice a day, for a week. It removed the skin but left the bugas.

The second remedy was to wash my face with the monthly blood of a virgin. I didn't try this method, so I can't say if it worked or not. I wonder what inspired the originator of this idea to think of it? I can picture him with a face full of bugas, feeling more depressed each day, sick of hearing "Joe, naay bugas" from everyone he met. I can see him spending days and nights in silent contemplation by the side of a river, searching for the answer to his bugas problem. While all of this is clear, I can't make the jump from this scene by the river to Joe suddenly leaping to his feet and saying, "Eureka! I'll use the monthly blood of a virgin!" And then there's the problem of having to collect it. Would he knock on doors and say, "Excuse me, Miss, but are you a virgin?"

What I finally did to solve my problem was to write to the Peace Corps health staff and request some of what I'd used as a student. This arrived within a few weeks, and by the following month my bugas were under control. When my neighbors noticed the change, they asked if I'd been using the soap. When I replied, "No," they laughed and asked who, then, was the virgin. I said, "You wouldn't know her. I had to get one from a far away village because I couldn't find any here."

Where's Brownie?

I spent much of my vacation time sitting on my porch reading Thoreau. On one afternoon, JoJo, Ayeng's oldest boy, came to my hut and presented me with a bowl of stew. While he was walking back down the trail to his hut, I called out and asked him what it was. "Dog," he said, and then smiled. I smiled too and waved goodbye. He was that kind of kid – always fooling, always into some sort of mischief. He was constantly making jokes or playing tricks, and he was constantly being scolded for them. Still, the harshest reprimand left him unfazed; he was a natural-born clown and would never change.

It may even have been Ayeng who was behind this joke. She had a playful streak in her, and I'd always suspected that she carried the genetic source of her son's clownishness. And she had reason for playing this on me. Just a few days before, while washing clothes, we started a talk which eventually turned to the river's leech population. In the middle of a sentence, I suddenly jumped up, pointed at her legs, and shouted, "Leech!" She leaped so high and started up such a leech-kicking dance that my insides hurt from laughter. True, a minute later I bested her leap when a real leech found my ankle, but I'd still tricked her. And this wasn't something she'd forget.

The stew – beef stew, probably – was as good as any I'd eaten. The bones were kind of small though – small and sharp – and this made me wonder if JoJo had really been telling the truth. Or was it just my imagination?

Well, I finished the bowl. I wasn't squeamish about eating dogs even though I'd always been a dog lover and had once vowed that I'd eat my fellow passengers on a life raft at sea before I'd eat, or let anyone else eat, my dog Rusty. But being in another country, living in a different way, and experiencing something new daily, I was in an exploratory frame of mind. Eating a stewed dog would neither change my vow to my deceased dog (who died from old age, I hasten to point out) nor reduce in any way my general love of the canine species. Rather, it would just be another one of a dozen new experiences that I'd had that week.

Also, the dogs in the Philippines weren't like the dogs back home. The people didn't view dogs as pets, but as food, and so treated them without the love and affection that we heap on our dogs. You don't treat something kindly that you will one day kill and eat; you can't do that if you're the one who has to kill and eat the animal.

All of the dogs that I ever saw – with just one exception – were dirty and disease-ridden nuisances. The exception was Beauty, Ayeng's dog. I'd played with her almost daily since she was a puppy. We used to chase each other around the fields by my hut. Beauty was the only "real" dog to me. She had a black, shiny, clean-looking coat, and a great smile – she *was* a beauty.

And it may be that it was my affection for Beauty that sent me to Ayeng's house later that afternoon. JoJo was a joker and was certainly playing a joke on me now, but I still had a twinge of doubt, and this was enough to send me out to check on Beauty. I would not have liked to have eaten her.

Ayeng answered my "Maajo" greeting call from her kitchen and told me she was cooking some bananas and would be right out. I put her stew bowl down and tried to relax in a chair. A few minutes later, my best pal Beauty came out from somewhere to greet me. I felt relieved, but only for a moment. Discomfort replaced relief when I began to realize that something was wrong. There was something wrong with the room I was sitting in – something different. It's disturbing to be sitting for the one-hundredth time in a room and suddenly feel like a stranger there. Something was out of place, and it was making me nervous.

Then it hit me: Where's Brownie? Brownie was the other dog – a miserable bugger who was always jumping up on things to get at somebody's dish of food. He was the antithesis of Beauty – dirty, ill-natured, greedy, and as pig-like as a dog will ever get. And he was the missing piece. Ordinarily, Brownie would have come charging out ahead of Beauty and gotten his dirty paw-marks all over my trousers and gotten his nose whacked out of the empty stew bowl a half dozen times. Where was Brownie?

Ayeng entered the room just as I'd thought this, and so my first words to her were, "Where's Brownie?" "You ate him for lunch," was her reply.

Serenade

I wasn't the only one on summer vacation. With the onset of the dry season, my farmer neighbors had free time as well. While I was using the evening time to read, write, and study the language, my neighbors were using the same time to drink tuba.

Before I began drinking with the farmers, I would often hear, "Maajo," the call which announced the presence of a visitor. These calls came between 10:00 p.m. and midnight, and I always knew what they were about before I opened my door: a group of drunken farmers had goaded one of their party – usually the drunkest – to go to my hut and borrow my guitar. I always gave it up with reluctance, for their parties could easily be heard from my hut; the addition of a guitar only increased the noise.

One night, I heard the "Maajo" call and thought, "Dang, they want my guitar again." At first I thought to play possum. The light from my candle wasn't very bright and so maybe the caller would think I'd gone to bed. But the calls continued and when I heard more than one voice, I opened the door to see what was up.

In the starlight, I could make out four dark figures. One of the shadows spoke and asked to borrow the guitar. I brought it out, but rather than thank me and leave, the men removed their slippers and climbed up to my porch. They seated themselves on my bench, put their coconut wine on the floor, and began singing and drinking.

I wasn't at all happy. First, I didn't know any of the men but one – and he was the village bully. Although he was a brute of a man, his name was Boy. He mistreated his sister and his kindly old father. He worked to get money for tuba, but that was the extent of his productivity. He was a genuine bogoy (a troublemaker and a mean man). The second reason for my unhappiness was that the men were so drunk that they could barely get the glass to their lips; my porch was stained a bloody red from the spilled wine. Third, they had to be the worst singers in the village. And fourth, I had something better to do; I used that time of night to write in my journal.

But this was still early in my service. Although I was definitely a part of the community, I was new enough not to want to offend anyone. So I waited as patiently as I could while they painted my porch red and pained my ears with their howls. I felt relieved when forty minutes later they all stood up, as at a signal, and stepped off the porch. But they weren't leaving; they just stood side by side for a group pee. In the dark, they couldn't see that they were standing in my vegetable garden.

When they returned to their drinking and singing, I made a mental note to talk this over with Ayeng. I had the lion's share of the two-year experience ahead of me, and I was not about to have my evenings wasted. Well, I grumbled on and on to myself, getting more sour by the minute. When I didn't think things could get worse, one of the men leapt to his feet, ran to the edge of the porch, and threw up over the stairs. He then walked through the vomit down the stairs and sat alone in the dark – as much out of embarrassment, I knew, as drunkenness.

But this vomiting had its positive side. It signaled the men that it was time to leave. And when the men reached the bottom of the stairs, they found that their friend had vomited on their flip-flops. So they had to squish their way home and in the morning would have a hell of a time erasing the red from the soles of their feet. All of this eased things for me. I was able to laugh and forgive the intrusion. I wasn't going to let it happen again, though, because I suspected that in the future my luck wouldn't hold out – that such evenings wouldn't end better than they began.

Tuba

I managed to avoid an encounter with tuba for the first six months of my service. Early on, I decided to tell my neighbors that I didn't drink. I thought that this would exclude me from invitations to the frequent drinking parties and so give me more time to use as I pleased. But after six months, near the end of my summer vacation when things were getting a little boring, I decided that one of the best ways to use my time was in drinking. As soon as word got out, I became a regular with the tuba crowd.

Tuba was the alcohol of choice in my village for several reasons. It was cheaper than any store-bought alcohol, its source was in the village itself, and there was a tradition to uphold: generation upon generation had partied on tuba, and this was reason enough to continue. Certainly the popularity of tuba had nothing to do with its taste. It was awful stuff, kind of thick and oozy and bitter – any more bitter and it would've been marketed as an emetic. Maybe my memories have been soured by the kind of tuba the farmers in my village drank: baho, aged tuba which was jugged and then buried in the ground. If left underground or on the shelf for too long, baho turned to vinegar.

Tuba came from the coconut tree – not from the coconut, but from the branches that fed the coconuts. A manangiti (tuba gatherer) was required to secure the stuff. This was usually a muscular man who, with a wooden tube strapped to his back and a machete at his side, would scale the trees using the toe holds which upon first assent were hacked into the tree and which were used on subsequent visits. The manangiti would battle through ants and bees and an occasional bird before settling into position amongst the branches at the top. Then he would choose his spot and, with machete, tap into the vein which ran through a branch. The liquid was gathered into the wooden tube, and when all was finished, the manangiti would return to the ground. He'd go from tree to tree tapping out the liquid until he had what he desired.

The clear liquid was mixed with tree bark which turned it a blood red color – difficult to get out of clothes, I found – and the finished product was called "tuba." And, as mentioned, it was the practice of the men in my village to bury this tuba, letting it age and grow in potency. The aged finished product was barely palatable for me, but my neighbors enjoyed it. Sometimes, for my benefit, they'd mix in a liter of coke which greatly improved the taste. Although I never refused their offer to add cola, I never requested that they do this. This was solely a move to save face, for usually only women drank tuba mixed with coke.

The men I drank with were farmers. The gatherings moved from hut to hut, each farmer hosting the party for a couple of nights every month. Everyone had his own tuba jug, which when dry was quickly run over to the manangiti's hut and refilled. Most of the gatherings took place at night. The men squatted outside the hut in a circle, though there were always one or two stools for the important guests. I never liked to be treated like a VIP in my village, but when faced with the choice between squatting for five hours or sitting on a stool, I always took the stool. I didn't have the Asian's ability to squat with feet flat on the ground. They could sit this way for hours without the least sign of discomfort. I, on the other hand, squatted on the balls of my feet and could keep this up for ten minutes tops.

In the center of the circle was a stool or a small table which held the jug of tuba and one glass. Someone – anyone but the man whose turn it was to drink – would fill the glass and slide it to the next drinker, and that man would continue conversing with the group until he'd been encouraged two or three times to drink. Five or ten minutes later, someone else would fill the glass and slide it to the next in line. This would go on all night – or at least for as long as the tuba held out. The only change to this ceremony came as the men grew drunker. As the hours passed, the time between receiving the glass and draining it was shortened, as was the time between draining the glass and refilling it.

A few hours into the drinking, when the gossip was on its second telling and when the men were drunk enough, someone would bring out a guitar. The guitar, like the tuba, would be passed about the circle. There were few men who couldn't play at least one song, and all of them had a favorite. And just as we were encouraged to drain our glass, so too was each man encouraged to sing.

I always let the others go first. Most sang Visayan love songs, which, in their drunkenness, they belted out with emotion. The singer's face would take on a pained look as he wailed about a lost love, a broken heart. Drunken voices reached pitches never attempted in sobriety, bringing laughter to their friends. At the end of the piece, the singer would always bow his head to his audience and say, in English, "Thank you very much." Laughter followed this, and the guitar was passed to another.

Not all of the songs were Visayan, though. Several farmers knew at least some of the words to the songs of "America's greatest singer": Matt Monroe. It wasn't until after I'd left the Philippines that I found out who Matt Monroe was – an old-time Canadian pop star. He must have been fond of recording the songs of Tom Jones and Englebert Humperdink because theirs were the songs that my neighbors attributed to Monroe. One Matt Monroe fan, the brutish man called Boy, would belt out "Delilah" when it was his turn. Since he didn't know any of the words, he would just wail out "LIE-LIE-**LIE**-DEE-**LIE**-LAH" again and again until he was joined by a half-dozen dogs.

I always managed to wait until either everyone decided to go home and sleep it off or until everyone was so drunk that they wouldn't care what I sounded like. I usually sang "Matud Mo" – an old Visayan love song that everyone knew well. With this song, I was usually able to talk two or three of the men into accompanying me and so let my voice disappear beneath theirs.

I remember most of my nights with the farmers, and I've never regretted my decision to join them. There's something about being drunk that evens things out. Neighbors who'd always been too shy to speak to the American were joking and laughing and telling me their best stories. Those who thought that my nationality or my appearance or my education made me better were able to see that I was just a man – a man who could get drunk enough to need a guide home, a man who was embarrassed to sing (and who had reason to be). Those were great nights – nights of learning, nights of connecting, nights of laughter.

A Boat Ride

As much as I enjoyed my time drinking with the farmers, I wanted to explore more of the Philippines before the summer vacation was over and I was back to presenting seminars. A few weeks of drunken nights with the farmers had improved my language significantly and those sessions, when supplemented by my own studies with my dictionary and Peace Corps language materials, moved me to a new level of comprehension. After six months, I could communicate effectively! I knew what to say, how to say it, and I was beginning to understand more and more answers regardless of length. I was feeling confident enough to take off and explore.

I hiked the hills above Dongon; I explored the remote villages across the river that separated my hut from the rest of the world, thereby frightening entirely new villages of children; I explored islands to the east, west, and south of Maasin; I traveled by bus to the northern part of the province and wandered around the main northernmost town. When I had had my fill of local sights, I traveled beyond the borders of Leyte Province.

Cebu Island, with its large airport, was my immediate destination whenever I wished to visit the rest of the Philippines, and it took a six-hour sea voyage to reach Cebu. Two of my many trips to Cebu are most prominent in my memory. One was when the sea got so rocky that I told myself that if I were ever going to get seasick, this would be the time. I managed to make it without paying tribute to Poseidon, but several of my fellow passengers were not so lucky.

But the trip I remember best came about because I just needed a break from being in the spotlight. I was tired of being stared at, pointed out, and followed, and so I sought to escape to another island. The trip to Cebu started out normal enough with the boat leaving the dock a few hours later than scheduled. They had the usual row upon row of cots, three feet by five feet with no support in the center, so you sort of sagged down in the middle with your head at the very top and your feet either dangling over the end or intruding on your neighbor's cot. No, there was nothing out of the ordinary here. The toilets still stunk so badly that you waited until everyone was asleep so you could take a leak off the end of the ship. The people aboard still stared at you – at your blond hair and white skin and hairy arms – until you closed your eyes and feigned sleep to shut them out. Nothing unusual here; instead, what keeps this ride in my memory is a group of college kids, their guitar, and their "Cutest Pop Songs of All Time" songbook.

There were four or five of them, boys and girls, huddled together in sing-a-long fashion not four cots away. I knew they were watching me as soon as I entered and claimed my cot. And when they started to sing, they all sat facing my direction. It was clear from their position and from the pitch of their voices that they were singing to, and for, me. Apparently they started on page one.

By page thirty I was as ready to kill another human – another four or five humans – as I have ever been and as I ever hope to be. I thought that what I ought to do was take fifty or even a hundred pesos, walk over to them, buy their songbook, and hurl that damn book as far out into the sea as my skinny arms could manage. Then I would return to my cot, close my eyes, and sleep in bliss, or, if not in bliss, then at least in silence. But I can't do that kind of thing. I'm the type of guy who'll imagine the rudest kinds of things but will always stop short of acting on them. What I did instead, then, was to sit up and glare. I gave them my best evil eye, my coldest stare. I imagined that I was ice – angry ice – and I shot icicle darts at their hearts. But my aim was off, for the songs and the smiles at me continued.

By page fifty I was sunk, and so I turned my ice-face away and stomped off to urinate. In my anger, I forgot to go fore or aft and so stepped into the foul-smelling bathroom by mistake. This, of course, only increased my anger at the minstrels; I was determined to go back and, with all the power of my inner spirit, will them to silence.

When I got back, I saw that they had visited my cot; a slip of paper – obviously foretelling doom – was sticking out of my backpack. I didn't want to read it. I shouldn't read it. *I mustn't read that scrap of paper.* But I read it anyway. I unfolded it, and, while all their eyes were on me, I read the words that I already knew would be there: "Hello. What is your name? We want to be your friends."

Game over. No more icy stares, and no more thoughts of murder and destruction. I put the paper in my pocket, gave my new friends a smile and a wave, lay back on the cot, closed my eyes, and listened until – somewhere around page seventy-two, I think – I drifted off to sleep.

On the Road: Sagada Cave

Once in Cebu, I could get to any place in the country. Cebu Airport had taken me to all of my Peace Corps meetings in Manila and had been my point of origin for numerous side trips: Boracay, Palawan, Gigante Norte, Bantayan . . . everywhere. During the final part of my summer vacation, I met John (a Volunteer buddy) in Cebu, and the two of us took off for the far north.

Banawe is known for its two-thousand-year-old rice terraces. But what I remember better is a wrinkled shirt. I don't know which fabric is the easiest to wrinkle, but take that fabric, squeeze it up into a softball, put it under the wheel of a steamroller, for a week, then put that shirt on and walk down the street. That's what the shirt looked like that the shoestring traveler had on when he walked by our table in the restaurant. When I saw the shirt, I said to John, "*That's* a wrinkled shirt." That shirt kept us laughing all morning and that's why the terraces, which I'm sure were lovely, are a blur, but the shirt's made a wrinkle in my memory.

We took a dusty jeepney ride from Banawe to Sagada. The other passengers, tourists from Europe, slapped their pant legs and watched the dust rise. We all laughed when I slapped my bare legs and got just as big a dust cloud. I can't remember if the ride was exceptionally long or if we just started out late in the day, but I know that when we arrived in Sagada, we went straight to a hotel and soon after to bed.

Neither of us slept more than a few minutes at a time because you'd just get yourself into the right position, and you'd just be spinning your way to that dream-filled REM sleep, when your ear would fill with a hum and you'd wake yourself up with a swat at your head. I don't know why people bother to swat at the mosquitoes in their ears; I've never known one to get a kill, and most times you just bang up your ear, or as happened with us, wake yourself out of sleep. Well, the swatting went on for some hours, and it wasn't long before it began to be accompanied by swearing in general and all sorts of grumbling about your noisy roommate when you were all safe but the skeeter was in his ear. After half a night of this, John and I finally did a wise thing (wisdom comes at the strangest hours and under the most stressful conditions): we turned on the lights and swayed around the room killing mosquitoes. There was not a buzz in the air at the end of twenty minutes, and we slept deeply for what was left of the night.

In the morning, after breakfast, we found ourselves hooked up with the same tourists who shared our jeep from Banawe. We decided to go through Sagada Cave together and save money by sharing the cost of a local guide. The guide was a young guy. He came equipped with a single rechargeable lantern. He led us to the entrance of the cave, stopped, put down his lantern, and said, "We're going in the cave. But first we'll smoke some hash." John and I abstained and, while the others smoked, discussed whether we should go through with the trip. As we'd already paid our share, we decided to stick it out. Our decision was both a mistake and a blessing.

It became apparent that we'd made a mistake when, deep into the cave, the lantern died and we were left hunched over in total blackness. The guide said to wait until he came back with another lantern. His words didn't cheer us a bit. All John and I thought about was that we were stuck in the middle of a cave, impossible to backtrack out of through the maze of crevices we'd crawled through and with no light to see by, and that our safety – perhaps our lives – depended on a stranger who was stoned. We had little hope that our guide would find his way back out safely, secure a decent lantern, and return to save us.

The only thing we felt relieved about was that we were in our right minds. I have no idea what it would be like to be standing in a black, damp hole with a head full of hash, but I suspect it'd be more frightening than groovy. We didn't learn anything from our companions; I can't remember them saying anything other than some quiet mumbles, which I took to be prayers in their own language. I was too frightened then to think of it, but it occurs to me now that that would have been the right time to let fly a boomer fart; the acoustics were perfect! It would have scared the hell out of our stoned companions, but it would have made John laugh, and we could have used some relief from the tension. Best of all, no one would know who farted – and even if someone guessed, you'd never see the finger they were pointing.

Well, we waited and we waited, losing confidence by the minute. John and I considered what to do if the guide didn't come back. It was impossible to find our way out. After standing in the blackness for ten or fifteen minutes, we didn't even know which direction we'd come from. If we'd headed off in the wrong direction, we could have easily been killed; it was a big cave and there were drop-offs everywhere. So we did the only thing we could do: we waited. And our guide returned. When the light shone and we saw he was coming, you could hear deep, emotion-filled sighs. What is strange is that we didn't have him lead us back out of the cave. I'm sure some of us – John and I at least – must have considered turning back at once, but this part is fuzzy in my memory; all I know is that we decided to push on.

And I'm glad that we did. Yes, we walked over, hunched around, and crawled through some jagged, slimy places. Yes, we all slipped on the rocks and cut our hands and legs. Yes, John didn't make one of the leaps and so was submerged in a pit of icy water. Yes to all of this and more, but when we reached our destination (which none of us had even known was our destination), when we reached the giant pool in the heart of the cave and took the six-foot leap which dropped us into the icy water (water which under any other circumstances you wouldn't even dab a finger in let alone submerge your entire body) – well, when we did that and had had our swim, it was all worthwhile.

The way out of the cave took much less time because our lantern stayed lit. It seemed far less dangerous retracing our steps. We fell down fewer times and were less bothered by the sharpness of the rocks, the sliminess of the walls, and the darkness of the cave. We emerged from the cave champions of a sort. We'd somehow done a wonderful thing, though we couldn't say exactly what it was that was praiseworthy. But there was something, and we did it, and that's how I remember it.

Hut Blessing

When I returned from my vacation-time wanderings in June, it was time to get back to work. I spent most of June and July developing seminars; afterwards, I hiked all around the district to deliver the lessons to the elementary and secondary teachers. In addition to the seminars, I gave demonstration lessons and lectured at the main college in town; I wrote articles for the division newsletter; I continued contacting book donors and built up the school libraries; I judged various speaking and recitation contests; and I assisted the local schools in any other way that they, or I, could think of.

My only focus other than work during those months was related to Thoreau. I'd continued reading and rereading *Walden*, and partly to genuinely share in Henry's experiences and partly because I was ready for a change, I decided that I wanted to build my own hut. As I hiked throughout the school district, I began to search for potential hut sites. The most promising spot seemed to be the far off village of Nonok Norte.

Nonok was beautiful. From the top of its hills, not only could I see the lands below, but I also had a good view of the surrounding mountains which were covered with coconut trees. Better still was the temperature; the noontime breeze was cool at such heights – not much chance of a bugas outbreak in those cool temps. The climate also had a magical effect on the vegetables. The marble-sized tomatoes that were grown in the lower hills were replaced by beefsteak-sized Goliaths in Nonok. I'd be in the mountains, it would be cool, and I'd have access to the best produce in the region. What more did I need?

Ayeng supplied the answer to that question. When I shared with her my plans for Nonok, she reminded me that I would be missed and that I had friends and neighbors who didn't want to see me go. And as to the building of the hut, well, if I had to have that experience, then I could build on a small piece of land that she and Nanding owned. "Look at the spot," she said, "and then decide."

I followed Ayeng as she walked down a path that led between her home and Nonong's hut, veered off the path through a small bamboo grove, and emerged on the other side in the middle of a kamote (sweet potato) field.

The field was bordered by bamboo on three sides and, most importantly, by a river on the fourth. The river below the kamote field was an offshoot of the same one that ran behind Nonong's hut. At the top of the bank, where the dirt ran down to the river border below, stood an enormous cypress tree, giant limbs stretching out over the bank and pointing in all directions. "You can live here," she said. "Nanding and his friend, Cerio, can help you build it. What do you think?" There was nothing to think about. The site was perfect, and best of all it was within a kilometer of my old hut, so my neighbors would remain the same. Ayeng had not only helped me find a new home, but she'd kept me from making a mistake by leaving the community that I'd finally become a part of.

Over the next four weeks, I spent time between seminars working on the hut with Nanding and Cerio. They were the builders; I was the helper. They cut down the bamboo, and I helped carry it to the hut site. While they laid the four wooden corner posts, I cleaned the bamboo by using a machete to slice off any new growth along each tall bamboo tree. While they did the carpentry that turned rounded bamboo poles into bamboo slats for the floor of the hut, I dug the pit for the outhouse. And while they did the artistic job of creating walls for the hut out of strips of young bamboo woven into a pattern known as *saa-saa*, I hiked to town to fetch nails, some rope, and a toilet for the outhouse. We finished the outhouse together, but Nanding and Cerio did the final job – the nipa roof – while I was giving a seminar in another village. All told, the hut cost me just about $100, and in comparing that amount with what I was paying to rent Nonong's place, I learned that Thoreau was right: it was far cheaper to own a hut than to rent one. And even though my friends did the bulk of the work – and nearly all of the expert touches – I made sure to include myself in as much of the work as they would allow me. It was my hut, after all, and the experience of building it was as valuable to me as the warmth and security that the hut represented.

It took just four weeks to finish the hut, so it was ready for occupancy in the first week of September in 1988. I was ready to move in immediately, but I was told that before I could do so, a blessing ceremony had to be performed. I didn't argue. I had found out early on how futile it was to argue about superstition with my neighbors. Here's what I mean. When I first started bathing in the river, groups of children would stand along the edge of the water and watch me. Maybe they were fascinated by my white skin, or maybe they just wanted to see how the American bathed. Whatever the reason, I began bathing in the evening to give me more privacy. But bathing near bedtime caused a stir. My neighbors warned that unless my hair was dry before I went to bed, I would go blind.

To tease them, one evening I walked down the village path with wet hair and announced that I was going to bed. The elders shook their heads and clucked their tongues and warned me again of the danger. In the morning, I sought out the tongue-cluckers and with a "so there" attitude informed them that I'd gone to bed with hair dripping wet and hadn't gone blind. Their answer to this was, "Ah, but you wear glasses, don't you?" And I couldn't get around that jab. It didn't matter that I'd worn them before I came to the Philippines. The people would just say that I'd probably gone to bed with wet hair in America, and that's when the eye trouble began.

Other beliefs, such as the one about sitting on stair steps being a precursor to marriage, also couldn't be attacked. I could sit on stairs for hours every day and a week later say, "How come I'm not married yet?" They would answer, "You will be," and, of course, they'd be right. So you have some understanding now of why I didn't argue about the hut blessing ceremony. I just gave my consent and agreed to meet at my hut at the break of day.

At 5:00 a.m., we were all there: me, Nanding, Cerio, and the two chickens. I didn't ask about the chickens. I knew from experience that such questions were usually answered without my having to say a word. Nanding led us into the kitchen, handed me a machete, and told me to cut one of the chickens – not to hack its head off, but to saw into the throat because they needed live chicken blood. I'd committed myself, and as there was no use in arguing, I went ahead and did the knife work while Nanding held the squawking chicken.

When the blood began to spurt, Nanding quickly carried the bird to my front door, wetted his fingers with the chicken's blood, and then used his fingers to draw a cross of blood on the door. Then he did the same on the kitchen door, in addition to dripping blood about the dirt floor. Finally, we walked over to the outhouse, some fifty feet away, did the same saw job on the second chicken, and drew a cross on that door. Nanding also dripped blood in and around the toilet. When that was done, Nanding assured me that now I wouldn't be bothered or visited by evil spirits, but had we not done the ceremony, he added, I would have received bad fortune throughout my stay in the unblessed hut.

The final step – more of a post-ceremony step – was to kill the still squawking chickens and submerge their bodies in a pot of boiling water. After the dunking, the chickens' feathers were plucked, the bodies were chopped into pieces, the pieces were fried over a fire, and then we had breakfast. End of ceremony.

Birds

My hut was built in the middle of a sweet potato field, bounded on three sides by bamboo groves and on the fourth by a river. At least a dozen coconut trees stood in the field. Their young coconuts fed me on occasion, but I grew more from watching the first light of day meet the coconut fronds, sending beams of new light over the field. My favorite tree was the lone cypress that grew between the bank of the river and my hut, for it was this tree, along with the shrimp, the eels, and the tiny fish in the river that attracted the birds.

I saw groups of sparrows every day. They weren't very colorful, and their song wasn't my favorite, but they were birds, they could fly, and they had a song; I was happy to have them for neighbors. More striking were the tikarols and the antolihaws. Tikarols – bright blue kingfishers – came almost daily to hover above the river and plunge in after a meal. I used to sit by the river to wait for them to come, and I never left the riverbank before they departed.

Antolihaws must be native to the Philippines because my dictionary defined them only as "a medium-sized yellow bird." They were banana-yellow – the solid yellow which makes for the most beautiful (but least tasty) banana. They didn't frequent my area as often as the tikarols. When one did come, it was in a rush. I'd catch a flash of banana-yellow out of the corner of my eye, and by the time I got a fix on the bird, it was on its way home.

There were owls too, but I never saw one. They'd make themselves known only on the darkest nights. They didn't "hoo" like owls are said to; they sounded more like "wak-wak." That's probably why my neighbors called them wak-wak. But "wak-wak" also meant "witch" – and the belief that owls were witches in disguise was what kept them from being eaten. I wished that the monkey-eating eagle (which once lived on my island) shared a dual personality which superstition protected.

There were chickens, of course. Chickens were everywhere – roosting in trees, scratching up gardens, running through houses, and getting run over by pedicabs and jeepneys. They'd scratch all around the sweet potato field outside my hut. They left the garden I'd planted alone, though; they seemed to know by instinct that nothing to sustain life was ever coming out of that plot.

Every morning, beginning at 3:00 a.m., I'd hear a dozen or more roosters singing "cock-a-doo-doo." I don't know what happened to the "dle" on the first "doo." Maybe that was their way of following the "Filipino Philosophy," as found in the belief that if one had enough to eat that day, then there was nothing to worry about. Maybe the roosters figured that if they could get by with a cock-a-doo-doo, why waste the effort on an extra syllable?

Over time, I learned to sleep through the 3:00 a.m. to 5:00 a.m. crowings, so the roosters didn't disturb me. And they were really pretty birds – much more beautiful than the ordinary hens. But on one day, I was most grateful for the presence of the plain-looking hens. I was sitting in my kitchen, mid-morning, either writing a letter or dashing off something in my journal, when I heard the chickens outside squawking. Squawking often meant that the roosters were all heated up, so I let it go. But when the squawking persisted, I sensed that something was wrong, and so I glanced out the open door.

There was a monster bird, five-foot wingspan, hovering ten feet above a group of frantic hens (the roosters were nowhere in sight). The bird's dark brown body and pure white head made it look like an eagle. I watched from my hiding spot behind the door as it lowered itself, grabbed a medium-sized hen, and carried it upwards. Fifteen feet into the air, it dropped the chicken, and so hovered back down again for another try.

I started to slide snake-like out of my doorway to get a clearer look, but the instant I moved, the bird was gone. From fifty feet away, he had spotted my movement and flown off towards a huge tree above the river. It would have taken me five minutes to walk to the tree, but the bird was there in five seconds with those huge beating wings of his. I ran down to the river thinking I could get another look at it. I wanted to see it fly; it was so beautiful. Of course it spotted me just as I reached the river, and it soared off again. It was gone from sight in a minute, but at least I got to see it fly again. I kept hoping it'd come back and take a chicken, but it never did. I would have killed a chicken myself and hung it from a tree branch just to see that bird swoop down and pick it up.

Henry Thoreau had a connection with the hawk; he likened himself to it, feeling that the freedom the bird expressed in flight was similar to a kind of freedom he felt within himself. I wasn't usually a superstitious person, but I liked to think that maybe I had just been paid a visit by the spirit of Thoreau. He was there to remind me that my experience in

Maasin was a spreading of my own wings and a symbol of my own beautiful flight.

Between the hawk, the invisible owls, the occasional antolihaw, the daily kingfishers, and the ever-present sparrows and chickens, I was able to hear some magical music and see some incredible sights. Every time I saw a kingfisher dive into the river, saw a banana-yellow antolihaw flash through the sky, or thought about the hawk and the hen, I knew I'd made the right choice in building my hut by the river. And, what's more, I knew I'd made the right choice in coming to the Philippines.

Snakes

Although I was still working with the schools and doing a myriad of presentations with different groups in the town, I spent all of my free time enjoying the hut. My first task was to organize my few belongings. I had so very little then (most of my clothing, dozens of books, and other belongings had been distributed throughout the village over time) that the task of moving in took no more than a few minutes. The water containers, the kerosene stove, and the desk and chairs fit snugly into the attached kitchen, while the remainder of my belongings – the clothes I had left, my favorite books, and my journal – fit into my backpack which I kept on a ledge above the one main room.

The room itself was about six feet by eight feet, and I went through the same routine every night at bedtime. First, I rolled out a mat woven from strands of soft bamboo, which just about covered the entire bamboo floor. Next, I laid out my "blanket" – a queen-sized blue sheet which I folded in half. I folded my spare sheet into a rectangle for a pillow. Then I put up my family-sized mosquito net, which had to be the best deal I made on any purchase ever. It held up without a tear for two years, and I used it every day. The preceding setup was done by kinki (a kerosene-filled lamp that was a housewarming gift from Dee) and, when all was prepared, I blew out the lamp and dived under the net. I usually fell asleep listening to the river music from the stream below my hut.

On the first morning after I'd finished arranging my belongings, I started my early-morning process of reversing what I'd done the night before. First, the mosquito net came down, was folded neatly, and was then stored on the shelf in my hut. Then the sheet was folded neatly and, along with the "pillow," placed in the proper place. All that was left was to roll up the mat, but as I began rolling it, out slithered a snake. It seems he'd been spending the night under one side of the mat, to the right of my feet. I was surprised to see him, but I wasn't really frightened. He was a puny fellow, perhaps two or two-and-a-half feet long, and not much thicker than a rope. I imagined him to be a youngster based on his appearance.

I carefully rolled up the rest of the mat and put it to one side of the hut. When that was done, I decided to get a closer look at my bedfellow. I wasn't crazy about snakes, you understand; it's just that I was in another land, and I was experiencing so many new things daily that I'd developed an exploratory side to my personality. Things that I would never have done back home, I did without a thought in the Philippines. And so when I woke up to find I'd spent the night with a snake, my first thought was to get to know him better. Remember, too, that he was just a puny little guy.

My guest, though, had spent all of his days in the Philippines, and he wasn't prepared to entertain any variation to his natural response to life's situations. So when I approached to get that better look, he at first attempted to slide away, but then, deciding I was too dangerous to take chances with, he stood up and faced me. When he stood up, I suddenly forgot there ever was such a place as the Philippines, and, with a rabbit's hop, I was back on the far side of the hut; with a second hop, I was out the door. But a minute later I was back inside, machete in hand.

I grabbed the machete because the snake stood up. I knew little about snakes, but I had seen movies and, as a boy, I had read the section on snakes in the encyclopedia. What the shows and the book told me was that snakes stand up when they want to strike and that certain snakes, the deadly cobra in particular, strike from this position. If my friend was a cobra, I had cause to be careful. I'd been told upon my arrival that cobras lived in the village. Several people told me the same story of the high school girl who was bitten near the bottom of the hill and died on her way to her family's hut at the top. This had happened not long before my arrival, so it was fresh in everyone's mind. But this wasn't the only story. It seemed that there were a few people from every section of the village who had died from a cobra's bite within the past five years.

I thought about this while I stood facing my intruder. My instinct to strike out at something that threatened me was checked, however, by a sort of all-purpose pacifism which I'd been toying with since I'd become a Peace Corps Volunteer and had started reading all kinds of Eastern scriptures. These books said to preserve life, to let the snakes and the spiders and even the mosquitoes alone. And, intellectually at least, I agreed with this. But in this instance, instinct stomped on the intellect.

I couldn't let the snake go because it might be that he was poisonous. And if he was poisonous, I didn't want him to make my hut his home. I had another year left of my Peace Corps contract, and I wasn't going to share my hut and risk getting killed. And I wasn't going to leave the hut to the snakes (by this time, I'd imagined a whole family of snakes – all offspring and siblings' offspring of my two-foot guest). It was a lot of trouble to build the hut, and it was my hut after all.

I don't think the sight of me brandishing my machete moved the snake to attempt an escape. Instead, I think he sensed that I was lost in my thoughts and so decided to make a slide for it. As soon as he moved, though, I was shaken from my "should I or shouldn't I" debate, took a quick step forward, and with one strong swing chopped the little fellow in half. I somehow knew that I'd better do this right the first time, and so I swung hard enough to need both hands to yank my machete out of the bamboo floor.

The snake, after only a little wriggling, died, but I waited for up to an hour to make sure that he wasn't playing possum. I'd clearly sliced him in half, but somehow the killing had increased my fear. Adrenalin was flowing, heart was pumping, mind was on vacation – and so I waited for an hour. And then, when I was absolutely positive he was dead, after much fearful poking, I picked up the snake and took him to Ayeng's house.

Nanding was home and so I told him of my snake experience and showed him the snake. And then I asked if the snake was poisonous. Nanding looked carefully at the snake, seemed to search for the best way to express his thoughts, and then gravely informed me that I'd just killed the deadly Tahi-Tahi snake. His news relieved me of any guilt I had from the killing. There was now no question in my mind that I'd done the right thing. I thanked Nanding, gave him the snake for his dog, and went triumphantly back to my hut.

While glorying in my prowess as a deadly snake annihilator, I decided to write up the adventure in my journal. When I got to the part where I'd learned both the name of my foe and its deadly nature, I got stuck on how to spell "Tahi-Tahi" and so consulted my Visayan dictionary. I found the following entry:

Tahi-Tahi: a harmless snake, much like the North American Garter; tahi: a slang word meaning "shit."

And so my swollen chest sank, and my ironing board back folded almost in half, for I'd been fooled once again by my comic neighbors. I crossed out the title of my journal entry – Deadly Snake Slain by Fearless Peace Corps Volunteer – and wrote in: I Killed a Shit Snake.

A Flood

The weather was never more important to me than when I lived in the Philippines. In the dry season, I had journal entries in which I recorded when the various sources of water – the rivers and drinking wells – dried up; these pages were followed by entries in which I recorded the fires that spontaneously erupted in the hills during the driest and hottest days. During those months, I had to hope along with my neighbors that at least one drinking source would remain full, and I had to make use of the little rain that came and added to the river by washing my clothes in the puddles that were left. In the rainy season – the rest of the year, that is – I wrote of knee-deep mud; of typhoons that brought never-ending rain; of the pile of dirty clothes that couldn't be cleaned in a muddy river or dried on a rainy day; and, of course, I wrote of the floods.

My hut was finished shortly before the really heavy rains began to kick in. When the daily downpours commenced, I was safe and dry in my leak-proof nipa hut. And, being situated ten feet above the water on a cliff-like bank, I had the best view for watching the rains pour into the river. But the sound was more impressive than the sight. The rains came down with such force that you became deaf to everything else. For those Volunteers who lived under tin roofs, it was a banging, clanging, crashing of water, and they must have thought that their roof was going to cave in at any moment. One of my friends, a deaf-education Volunteer who was deaf herself and could only hear certain pitches, had heard rain for the first time beneath a tin roof during a Philippine downpour.

Every day for nearly a month, I'd watched and listened to the rain from my hut's porch. The sounds aided my meditations, and I read and wrote and prepared my seminars in peace. But, as seems to happen with peaceful feelings, they depart as quickly as they arrive, and their cause for departure is the very thing which brought them. In my case, the continuous rains eventually raised the river to a dangerous level. I began to ignore my books and journal and instead sat staring at the rising river. The river continued to rise while I was awake, and it swelled and raged as I slept.

Right around the start of my second year in Maasin, the water from the never-ending rain had risen to within two feet of the top of my formerly safe bank. And with the passing of another day (and a very long night) of heavy rain, the water began to spill over the bank and flood my small garden. I was less concerned about my vegetables than I was about the hut, for even though the hut was built off the ground, I knew that it would only take another day or two of this nonstop rain to wash my hut down the river. The same thought struck my neighbors, and several of them stopped by to suggest that I move out while I still could. But I was a proud captain who was prepared to weather the storm, trust in fate, and let things be – at least for another night.

That night I awoke to the river music. The plops and swooshes that had always put me to sleep were now filling me with fear, for they were coming from beneath the bamboo slats that made up my floor. When I walked out onto my porch, I found that the sweet potato field, which surrounded my hut, was a foot deep in water.

By breakfast time, the river had covered my lower porch, which was about two feet off the ground. That left two more feet to the second porch, which was also the level of my bedroom floor. I really didn't know what to do. I still wanted to wait out the flood. I still had some hope that it would end. So instead of leaving, I prepared to leave. I moved all of my possessions into neat piles on the floor of my room. I had already taken everything out of the kitchen – which sat at ground level and had a dirt floor (which was now a river floor) – and moved it all to my upper porch. When my bedroom things were packed, I was ready if I had to evacuate.

That afternoon, Nanding and Cerio waded out to my hut and told me that it was time to move. I didn't argue. A downpour had been in progress all day, and I knew there was no hope. The water was just inches below my bedroom floor, and at any time the dirt beneath it could wash out and send my hut down the river. I'd already seen dozens of coconut trees washed down. They were growing along the riverbank, and the ground beneath their massive roots melted away, making them firewood for the people downstream. If the mighty coconut trees could fall, then there was no hope for my puny one-and-a-half room bamboo hut.

We moved all of my possessions in a few minutes and stored them in Cerio's hut, which was well back from the river. Nanding told me that I would spend the night in his house. On the way to his place, as we passed my hut, I noticed a gathering of people. Ayeng was among them, so I stopped and asked her what it was all about. She answered that the people were gathered to see if my hut would float down the river or not. I stayed then. I was the owner, the captain, and even if I wasn't going to go down with my "ship," then I at least thought that I ought to be on hand when it made its maiden voyage. I stayed and watched – watched the waves break around the hut, watched as more coconut trees came spinning down the river, watched as part of my beloved cypress tree broke apart, joined the rest of the debris, and sailed off. When it was too dark to see anymore, I left for Ayeng's place. The hut, at that time, was still standing.

That night I shared a room with Nanding and his two boys. The three of them took one bed against one wall, and I had the second bed on the other side of the room. I couldn't sleep. The hut was on my mind. In front of my neighbors, I kept calm. When they asked me how I felt, I replied: "If it goes down, it goes down. No problem." But that night I lay awake wondering what I was going to do if I found myself hutless in the morning. I loved that hut. It was the first thing in my life that I had helped to build, and it was my sanctuary – my hermitage – the only place in Maasin where I could go and truly be alone for a few minutes. Those thoughts and more kept me from sleep.

I was also kept awake by a leak in the roof. It wouldn't have been so bad if I hadn't been under a mosquito net, for whenever a drip dropped, it would hit the net and branch out into a dozen mini-sprays. And I couldn't remove the net because I'd be swarmed by the mosquitoes. When I did manage to drop off, late into the night, I had a nightmare. All I can recall is that I was being pursued by several men. They were chasing, and I was dodging, and just as they were about to pounce on me, I woke up yelling. Nanding and the boys woke up too, and I spent the rest of the night sitting Indian style in the driest corner of the bed, keeping myself awake, avoiding dreams, and letting the others get some rest.

At daybreak, I let myself out of the house and made my way down the muddy path to my hut. The rain, I noticed, was just a regular rain – definitely not a downpour. This gave me some hope that the worst hadn't occurred. My flight was slowed when I came to the submerged board which lay across a small river, an offshoot of my river. I had to first extend a foot and feel for the submerged board. When I'd found it, I inched myself along its length until I made it to the mud on the other side. I sloshed through the mud with quickening steps until I reached the path outside the bamboo grove which led to my hut. It was here where the people had gathered to watch my hut wash away. And it was here that I alone in the early morning hours saw my hut, undamaged, standing just as I had left it.

The light rain continued throughout the day, but the floodwaters lowered. And against all advice to wait out another day, I spent that night in my empty hut. I had an overwhelming sense of relief. I knew that if the hut wasn't taken the night before, then it wouldn't be taken at all. The water beneath my floor did nothing to affect my sleep that night. All was well. The captain was back. He should never have abandoned ship. And, just as I knew, in the morning the water was down. It would continue to fall despite the persistent light rain.

Although I would like to end this memory on a positive note, I have to add a short postscript. When the flood waters retreated and my belongings were returned to the hut, I noticed for the first time the main casualty of the flood: my outhouse. The outhouse was a good fifty feet from the hut and being no more than a concrete seat resting on a few boards above a pit six feet deep, it wasn't sturdy to begin with. The door was gone, but this was minor compared to the ground beneath the bowl which had washed out, leaving a teetering bowl supported by a few warped and rotting boards.

For the duration of my stay, I continued to use the toilet in its weathered condition. And though it managed to hold out, I never once used it without fearing that this would be the time that the support beams would give way, sending me and my naked behind into the pit below.

The Rice Story

When the rains abated and I was back in my hut, I returned to my usual routine of working with the schools and of watching for the sunny days that interspersed the long rains so that I could do my laundry or else continue my exploration of the surrounding hills. I'd now experienced both dry and rainy seasons, drunken nights with the farmers, a host of critters, and unusual meals. In addition, by the end of my first year, I was fluent in the language. Certain events had helped to catapult me into fluency, among them the hut break-in (where I had to discuss the event over and over), the tuba nights (where I talked and joked with the farmers), and the building of the hut (where I had daily conversations with Nanding and Cerio). With the language mastered, the last of the strangeness disappeared, and I was beginning to think that the regular surprises that had greeted me every day of my first year were done. And then I found the canister.

It was morning, and when I stepped outside my hut to stretch and enjoy the sunrise, I saw the tall tin canister on a nearby stump. When I opened it, I found it to be two-thirds full of uncooked white rice. Although I may have complained that another possession was the last thing I wanted, I was secretly happy to have such a sturdy container, and I wished I knew who the friend was who'd left it for me. I guessed that it was Ayeng. She was always having something sent over – a bunch of bananas, a bowl of stew, a young coconut.

I carried the canister, not without difficulty for it was heavy with the weight of the rice, and set it on my kitchen table. I took my own sack of rice down from the nail in the roof where I'd hung it from a kerosene-soaked rope to keep it clear of bugs. Now that I had this sturdy canister with its lid, I wouldn't need the rope or the nail; I could keep the rice right on my table beside the rice pot and the gravity-fed kerosene stove.

I opened the sack and emptied the large rice kernels into the canister. I bought wild rice, or "red rice" as my neighbors called it, because I'd learned in Peace Corps training that it was more nutritious. My neighbors, however, never ate it, and I can't recall having eaten it anywhere but in my hut during my two years in the Philippines. With the addition of the red rice, the canister was now nearly full.

That afternoon, Ayeng paid me a visit. She was there, I knew, to see that I'd received the rice. Before I could thank her, she asked me if I'd found a container near my hut. She said it was left there by Abeth, a neighbor, and that it was a repayment of rice that Ayeng and her family had lent to Abeth's family some months ago. At the crack of dawn, Abeth had carried the rice as far as my hut when it started to rain. She set the watertight canister on the stump and ran back to her hut, thinking that she would take it over later in the day. Too embarrassed to say that I'd thought the rice was for me, I opened my kitchen door and gave the canister to Ayeng. She thanked me and carried it to her home.

For dinner that night, I ate my emergency rations: raisins and peanuts, in addition to a few bananas. I almost always had bananas around, and sometimes five or six of them made up my lunch or supper. These rations, along with several glasses of water, filled me up enough so that a few hours later I was able to fall asleep on a relatively full stomach.

It must have been 11:00 p.m. when the calls of "Maajo! Maajo!" woke me up. It was Nanding who, without a word, handed me a covered bowl and then left. I uncovered the bowl and found it filled with steaming rice and a large piece of fish. I wasn't hungry, but I ate it all, knowing that between the heat and the insects, it might not be as palatable in the morning. I went to bed wondering why this meal came at all, and why it was sent at 11:00 p.m.

The next morning, when I went to Ayeng's home to thank her for the meal and to return her bowl, I found my answers. After arriving home with the canister, Ayeng dumped it into a huge basket which contained the family's yearly rice. She was surprised to find the red rice mixed with the white rice, and throughout the day and on into the night, the presence of the red rice was the main topic of conversation in her household. It wasn't until bedtime that Nanding, still milling over the mystery in his mind, realized that the red rice must have come from me, and from that realization, he and Ayeng were able to piece together how I had managed to fill their canister with my own rice.

And with the solution to the puzzle came pity, for to a Filipino, if you have not eaten rice with a meal, then you have not eaten. And so at that late hour, Ayeng cooked a pot of rice and warmed up the fish that she had salted and stored for the family's morning meal, and Nanding ran it over so that I would not have to go to bed without having eaten that day.

Inko Tikoy Straightens His Back

The path from my hut to the rest of the world passed bamboo groves and rice fields. Just before it ended at the main road, which led in one direction to the town and in another to the far off mountain villages, it passed Inko Tikoy's hut.

Inko Tikoy was an old man with a bent back. It wasn't a crooked back; he had a perfectly straight back, which instead of rising up from his waist, projected forward, parallel to the ground, so that he resembled an ironing board. I'd seen several old folks with similar backs but none so far gone as his. I'd heard that the backs were caused by the short brooms that everyone used; in order to sweep, you had to adopt a bent-back posture. As huts and yards were swept every morning, and as Inko Tikoy was an old man, I figured he must have done an awful lot of sweeping in his lifetime. And he was still at it. Every morning he was out sweeping the yard or else he was bent over tending his garden. I thought that his posture may have made it easier to do these chores, but it looked painful.

When not sweeping the yard, he was always seated on a bench on his porch, bent back pushing his torso forward. He sat facing the road, and if he lifted his head up high enough, he could watch the pedicabs and jeepneys that occasionally passed by. He'd watch me as I returned from my shopping or from my excursions into the hills, and he'd always perk up and greet me. But unlike most of the people I passed on my walks, he never tried to keep me with idle talk. He'd give a wave, say hello, and let me pass. Then I'd go my way, and he'd go back to watching the road.

As months passed, I got to like Inko Tikoy and his quiet manner so much that I began to stop and chat with him. I'd ask him about his garden and how he grew his vegetables, and whenever I received pictures of my family, I shared them with him. I respected him for his industry and his silence, and he seemed happy with the attention I showed him. But my favorite memory has nothing to do with his gardening or our daily meetings; instead, it has to do with a visit.

After I'd been away from home for a year, my father took time out from one of his business trips to visit me at my site. It took a two-hour plane ride from Manila, a six-hour overnight ship ride, and a pre-dawn hour's hike into the hills, but my father made it. He only had till lunchtime to visit (Dad was obviously a stranger to Filipino time), so I showed him around, demonstrated how I bathed, how I washed clothes, and how I prepared meals. While I was giving him the tour, a neighbor climbed one of the coconut trees and brought down some young coconuts for my father to try. After he'd tasted one, it was time to leave.

Arriving as early as we did, we passed by Inko Tikoy's hut before he was up, but he was sitting at his spot on the porch when we went back out to the road. I brought my father over to meet him. Inko Tikoy was delighted at having the honor of meeting my father – someone whom he regarded as being far above him on the social ladder which all Filipinos are conscious of. When my father extended his hand in greeting, Inko Tikoy raised himself off the bench and, with the help of his left hand (which he rammed into the center of his back and held there like a brace), stood up as straight as he could. In this position – which was obviously more painful to him than the ironing board posture – he extended his hand and shook my father's vigorously. This was a great day for Inko Tikoy – a day to be remembered. I know that I always will.

The Days Race By

The second year of my Peace Corps service passed by in a flash. Time had speeded up when I shifted from presenting seminars to participating in the post-testing of the district's elementary and secondary students. The testing took me away from my site for a long stretch of time as I hiked with an administrative team to the farthest villages to administer the tests.

Our journey began where the public transportation stopped: Nonok Norte, the spot where I had once considering settling. From Nonok, we followed small paths that took us to the most remote regions of the area. The scenery beyond Nonok was beautiful: green everywhere, coconut trees in all directions, and our immediate path was lined with newly growing banana trees and abaca plants. The path ended some hours later in the tiny village of Libertad, which was the last village in the district. I was unknown there, so the few people of the village gathered together and stared at the stranger from a great distance, too shy and frightened to come near me. However, it only took a few words in Visayan and some smiles to make the crowd warm to me, and I left the village with new friends.

Over the next weeks, we would hike through rain and shine to tiny villages sprinkled throughout the high hills – to Hinapu-Daku, Tigbawan, Basak, and Cabagdiangan, the highest point in Maasin. Cabagdiangan was so small that the entire school system was comprised of two grades: first and third. The following school year, the grades would shift to second and fourth to accommodate the small student population, and then it would return to first and third for the following year. If the students needed additional education, they would have to travel to another village.

In one of these two-teacher villages, while the other administrators were testing, I borrowed a piece of paper from one of the teachers so that I could write a letter. The paper turned out to be her last, though. I didn't know this until later when I asked for a second piece. She had none to give me – not even scrap paper. I told her to forget it, but I think she felt ashamed, so she borrowed a sheet from the other teacher and presented it to me with great ceremony. The further out we went – and this was the furthest – the fewer the materials, supplies, teachers, students . . . you name it.

The hikes throughout the high hills were the highlight of my second year. I was doing what I liked best – walking – and in a place that was Edenic in beauty. Each trail led to a more beautiful place – a solitary coconut grove, a mountain stream with not a soul in site, a single bamboo hut on the edge of a kamote field. These were my views during those weeks. And when we reached Cagnituan, I knew that I had found the most beautiful place in Southern Leyte.

Cagnituan was the tiniest village, consisting of a handful of huts that were mainly grouped around the most level piece of ground in the area. While the people there were mostly typical Filipinos, I met a man from a clan known as the Managas (meaning "tall men"). He was over six feet tall! All of the Managas, I learned, were tall and had handsome features. None of my companions could tell me of the ancestry of the Managas, but they did increase my curiosity by telling me of a fair-skinned branch of the family.

However, it wasn't the Managas that made Cagnituan special to me; instead, it was the waterfall which emerged from a huge cave and fell over rocks into a natural pool below. I went swimming in the pool with two of the men from the village, and then later we climbed up the waterfall's rocks and made our way into the water-filled cave. We walked until the cave's water reached our chins, and then we swam the rest of the way in. We held our flashlights above water with one hand until we reached some high rocks above the level of the water. From the rocks, we shined our flashlights upward and watched the bats and swallows. We investigated the stalagmites and stalactites and then returned to the waterfall below, swimming in and under its connecting pool, before heading back to the village. The hike to Cagnituan was a perfect way to end the school year. With my second summer vacation at hand, and with an active travel bug from my wanderings in the hills with the administrators, I decided to explore as much of the Philippines as I could squeeze in.

I made a return trip to the mountain provinces to the north; likewise, I returned to Cebu City and its surrounding beaches. For new discoveries, I broke a Peace Corps rule and explored Mindanao, the stronghold of the New People's Army. While I didn't see any NPA, I did find a half-dozen towering waterfalls at Cotabato, wild monkeys at the tops of trees in far off Tawi-Tawi Island, and fruit and other delicacies found only in the southernmost areas of Zamboanga to the west and Davao to the east. From March to June, I was either en route to, returning from, or in the process of exploring some distant site; thus, the three months of summer vacation, like my travels through the high hills of Maasin, passed by like a blur.

When I finally returned to my hut for the start of yet another rainy season, I did so with the realization that the adventure would soon be over – that I had, in fact, just five months of service remaining. I wanted to spend those last months with the people I cared the most for, so I decided to rearrange my schedule. I did less seminar work and instead used that time to co-teach with Ayeng. I'd spend my mornings with her and the students of the village, and then I'd hike to town to visit with Fe and Dee. In the evening, I was with Nanding and the tuba crowd, drinking, singing, and telling jokes late into the night. In between these main parts to my final days, I would sit by the river and listen to its music, or I would record my thoughts and experiences in my journal on the porch of my bamboo hut. I knew that when it would be time to go, I wouldn't have any regrets; there would be nothing I'd wanted to do that I hadn't done and no one I cared for that I hadn't shared time with. When it was time to leave, I would be ready.

Sweet Chariot

It was almost time to leave, and there was one task left undone; I was determined to correct that one blemish before I'd left Maasin forever. The blemish had to do with what, for me, was the most dreaded aspect of Filipino culture: the singing. Filipinos are natural-born songsters. Every seminar I conducted had to open with a group song. Every break required games and more singing. Finally, we had the end-of-seminar singing. This last was the worst, what I really dreaded, for it required solo performances. Singing songs with neighbor men too drunk to remember anything in the morning was in no way preparation for daytime sober solos in front of twenty female teachers.

I had no trouble with the group songs because I'd had a lifetime of practice mouthing songs – from my first days at Sunday school to every public school event that involved singing, and even to college where the volume of the speakers at the discos made it impossible to know who was singing along. But these solos were to be feared. They worked as follows. At the close of the seminar, everyone would be corralled into a room – usually the home economics room – and after snacks, the encouragement would begin. The first to be pressured into a song was always the teacher with the sweetest voice. The pressure from the group would be met with strong protest, which prompted more pressure and more protests (weaker this time), until eventually the teacher stood up and did what she'd wanted to do in the first place: sing her heart out. The repeated refusals were all part of the game, part of the culture.

I was the only one who protested in earnest. Whenever the pressure was turned on, I did whatever it took to weather it without yielding. Once, in April, I got around it by playing "Silent Night" on the harmonica. Other times I would juggle bananas. But by far my most often used technique was humor: I told every group of teachers I worked with that I couldn't possibly sing with so many coconut trees around. When they asked what I meant, I replied that my voice would surely bring coconuts raining down on their heads. While they were laughing, I grabbed my teaching gear, stashed my "bring house" (the meal leftovers apportioned me), and headed for the door.

I knew this technique couldn't work forever. One day the teachers of a village school would be ready for my coconut story and have the exits blocked. Also, it was such an important part of the culture that I knew I just had to do it. For two years my friends and coworkers had pleaded with me to sing, and for two years I had turned them down. So, in preparing for that fateful day, I wrote a letter home and asked for a copy of "Swing Low Sweet Chariot." I chose that song because, to my unmusical ear, it seemed to be usually sung in a low and relatively unvaried pitch. I'd known from the few sober times I'd sung above a whisper that I couldn't alter pitch without sounding as if I were on my deathbed in the final stage of some horrendously painful disease. So I knew for certain that if ever I sang, it would have to be something low and steady. And it wasn't long before the lyrics arrived, and I had the "opportunity" to give the people what they wanted.

The day came, as I had feared. I'd had the lyrics for some time, but still I had waited until my very last seminar to join in. At that late hour, I still considered juggling or joking my way out of it, but when the pressure to sing was poured on, I gave in and took my place in front of the room (which was far fuller now than when we'd started the seminar, for no sooner had I agreed to sing than a fleet-footed teacher had dashed out and brought in everyone outside to hear the singer from America).

With a packed classroom, I lost all of the nerve that got me up there. But it was too late to back down, so I began – a cappella. The room, which was pin-drop silent, began to fill with my song, which I found I had going at a much higher pitch than I'd practiced; the fear I felt carried my voice to soprano. Also, there was a noticeable tremor running beneath the words, which I hoped my audience would interpret as a Western-style vibrato. I got through two verses and then quit, deciding in the middle of the song that if anyone complained of the brevity, I would insist that that's as long as the song was and that I'd done my part.

No one complained. No one made any noise at all. And it's hard to describe how they looked. The closest I can come is to say that each teacher had a look of pity, sickness, embarrassment, pain, and sorrow all rolled into one. When I'd reached my seat, there was still no reaction. Eventually, a kind teacher, whose pity must have outweighed her horror, began to clap. This woke the others out of their bewitched state, and they too joined in. Then the party ended even though there were still others who hadn't had their turn.

It wasn't how I'd imagined my final goodbye would be, but, upon reflection and with the help of twenty years to lessen the impact of the experience, I can today say with certainty that it was an appropriate end.

I'd gone into Maasin as green as could be, each day producing one embarrassing moment after another until I felt certain of just two things: one, that such moments were reserved for me alone and two, that there was a limitless supply of such moments. But the plus side to it all was the stories that I left for my neighbors to enjoy. Even today, so many years later, I am certain that somewhere in Maasin sits a group of teachers, or some students grown old, or perhaps a group of men passing around the tuba jug who are remembering the "Peace Corpse" who fought with a flying cat, whose body swelled up with every bug bite, who wandered the high hills looking for a virgin for his bugas, and whose voice could make the coconuts fall from the sky.

Post Peace Corps

At the end of their service, some Peace Corps Volunteers travel with the money from the small readjustment allowance they're given, some get married either to villagers or sweethearts back home, some stay on for another year, and some go back to the U.S. to begin graduate school, to return to their old jobs, or to begin a new job. I went home and did nothing. Well, almost nothing.

I spent the month of December at home, talking and drinking with one friend whenever he was free. Otherwise, I mainly kept to myself, sidestepping questions from family and friends about what I was going to do next. The choices seemed to be graduate school or work. I left a world where every moment of every day seemed to offer an infinite number of novel experiences; back home, I had two choices. I left a town where I was an important part of the community – someone who everyone knew and connected with on some level. Back home, I was nobody. Everything that was once familiar to me was now foreign, and I felt like my real home was in Maasin and not in the United States where I had grown up. But I had left the Peace Corps – finished my contract – and I felt like I could not go back.

After about a month, just as the 1980s made way for the 1990s, I left home and began to wander. I drifted to Florida, where I lived hermit-like in a condominium for a few months. From there, I traveled across the country, sometimes stopping to stay with an old friend for a day or two. In the summer, I used the very last of my Peace Corps readjustment allowance to travel to Taiwan, where I worked as an English teacher. Every penny I saved fueled my future wanderings: a month or two back in the United States, bus rides across Mexico, and four or five months of hitchhiking and walking from Guatemala all the way to Costa Rica. By the summer of 1991, I was back in the United States for my sister's wedding. A few days later, I was on a one-way flight back to Taiwan, where I intended to rebuild my cash reserves before losing myself in the jungles of Sumatra in Indonesia. For the most part, I had been living out of a small tent, which I carried in a backpack with the rest of my few belongings: a notebook to collect my thoughts, a copy of Thoreau's *Walden*, a toothbrush, and two changes of clothing. I never made it to Sumatra. Instead, I met a woman who made me think about how I had been living and what I had been missing since leaving the Peace Corps.

After spending the very last of my money to rent a room for a month in a shared apartment in Taipei, I walked around the campus of National Taiwan University looking for places to post advertisements of myself as a private English teacher. I could not speak the language or read any signs and ended up wandering into a girls-only dormitory. I was stopped two feet into the compound by a female guard who took a full five minutes to scold me. Or at least that's what I think she was doing; the frown, the barking tone, and the popping forehead veins were my only clues.

In the middle of my humiliation, a young student, who was pedaling home from her classes, came to my rescue. In broken English, she explained where I was and why I shouldn't be there, and she walked me out and directed me to the main billboard where I could place my ads. But when the ads were posted, neither one of us wanted to say goodbye. After that first day with Yee-chen, and five more like them, I realized what I had really been doing for the past year since leaving Maasin.

The tent had become my surrogate hut, and the few things I kept within my backpack represented my attempts to re-create the simple lifestyle I maintained in the Philippines. My time in Mexico, Central America, and Taiwan moved me closer to my Peace Corps experience by placing me in foreign lands with foreign languages and different cultures. But there was one main difference: in the Philippines, I belonged and I was loved. In my life after the Peace Corps, nowhere felt right, and I was lonely all of the time.

Yee-chen was the missing piece. She was a foreigner in Taiwan, having grown up in poverty as an ethnic minority in Burma. What I had experienced for two years with my hut and outhouse, my river washings, and my bowls of rice, Yee-chen had experienced her entire life. While I had taken some of my two years to skim what I could from Eastern philosophy, she had grown up in a village steeped in Taoist traditions. She was the community and the love that I had been missing for more than a year. For her, I was the young man that she had known as a child – the one with the blond hair who came to her in her dreams. I was the one who in real life wanted to know what she thought. I was the one who saw how beautiful she was.

A week after meeting, we decided to marry; a week after the decision, we were husband and wife. We had created a miniature Peace Corps experience: two persons from disparate cultures and languages who have not just two years but a lifetime to learn about one another, to help one another, and to grow from the experience.

Twenty Years Later

I trace everything good in my life back to the Peace Corps. This summer Yee-chen and I will celebrate our 19th wedding anniversary. That's not bad for a couple who married a few days after meeting. I often think about how we never would have met if it hadn't been for the Peace Corps and my life in Maasin. I never would have visited Taiwan if I hadn't already experienced life in another culture and if I hadn't lived just to the south in the Philippines. I guess if I hadn't been a Peace Corps Volunteer, I wouldn't have been able to locate Taiwan on the map.

And if the Peace Corps led me back to Asia, where I met my wife, then it was also responsible for our son who was born while Yee-chen and I were living in Guam a few years after marrying. Along with Yee-chen, Ray – who is now 15 years old – completes my small universe. In a household steeped in both Asian and American cultures and languages, Ray has grown into a happy human being who can shift easily between East and West.

My profession, too, is a result of my Peace Corps experience. I graduated from college with a degree in English. When I left the United States for Maasin, I had zero training in working with non-native speakers. After two years of working exclusively with that population, I found a way to connect all of my future jobs with non-native speakers. In Taiwan, I taught Chinese students and trained teachers. In Guam, I taught students from all over Micronesia. After having lived for 10 years in Asia and Micronesia, we returned to the United States, where I taught both foreign students (in a middle school) and migrant farmers (at a migrant center). Later, I worked with teachers who served exclusively on Native American reservations. Still later, I worked in school districts and language academies with a focus on culturally diverse non-native speakers of English. My last job had me working with teachers-to-be so that they would know how to care for their own second language learners in Florida's public schools.

My family and my career have sprung out of my Peace Corps experience. Even my doctorate came through the Peace Corps after I became the first Peace Corps Doctoral Fellow at Northern Arizona

University in Flagstaff. But the influence is greater still. When I meet someone in the market who looks different or sounds different, I do not view that person with suspicion and quickly walk away. Instead, I move closer and ask *Where are you from?* and *What language do you speak?* I want to know their story. I want to see where we meet and where we differ. I am who I am today because of my two years in Maasin. I am grateful for what I have received, and I very much want to pay something back. Perhaps with this book I have moved ever so slightly towards paying back that wonderful debt.

About the Author

Dr. Gary Robson started his career in education as a Peace Corps Volunteer in the Philippines. Between 1987 and 1996, he taught K-12 students and trained teachers in Asia and Micronesia. Since 1996, Dr. Robson has worked in various educational settings within the United States. Although his area of expertise is ESOL (English for Speakers of Other Languages), he has worked with a variety of students and has taught multiple subjects in a number of settings. *Misadventures in Maasin* is his second book. *Chess Child*, his first book, tells the story of his son, Ray Robson, and how he became America's youngest grandmaster.

To learn more about Dr. Robson and his upcoming projects, visit www.NipaHutPress.com.